D0470286

GOD'S AMAZING CREATION

GENESIS 1-2

KAY ARTHUR
JANNA ARNDT

HARVEST HOUSE PUBLISHERS

EUGENE, OREGON

Scripture quotations in this book are taken from the New American Standard Bible ®, © 1960, 1962, 1963, 1968, 1971, 1972, 1973, 1975, 1977, 1995 by The Lockman Foundation. Used by permission.

Illustrations by Steve Bjorkman

Cover by Left Coast Design, Portland, Oregon

Harvest House Publishers, Inc., is the exclusive licensee of the federally registered trademark DISCOVER 4 YOURSELF.

Discover 4 Yourself® Bible Studies for Kids

GOD'S AMAZING CREATION

Copyright © 2001 by Precept Ministries International
Published by Harvest House Publishers
Eugene, Oregon 97402
www.harvesthousepublishers.com

ISBN 978-0-7369-0143-7

All rights reserved. No part of this publication may be reproduced, stored in a retrieval system, or transmitted in any form or by any means—electronic, mechanical, digital, photocopy, recording, or any other—except for brief quotations in printed reviews, without the prior permission of the publisher.

Printed in the United States of America.

09 10 11 12 13 14 / ML-BG / 13 12 11 10 9 8 7

For Silverdale Baptist Academy, 2000–2001
Mrs. McCoy's fifth-grade class:

Brent Arndt	*Sarah Axley*	*Tiffany Baker*	*Christopher Chilton*
Jordan Eaves	*Amy Farrow*	*Jonathan Patterson*	*Zach Pinter*
Robby Ratledge	*Starla Stafford*	*Joy Tanner*	*Chris Twitty*
Katherine Twitty	*Philip Walliser*	*Jackie Rae Wright*	

You are awesome! I can't wait to see how God is going to use each one of you as you continue to study His Word and walk in His ways—2 Timothy 3:14-15.

For my son Brent (the real-life Max), my imaginative storyteller, whose dreams fill my life with fun and adventure—Philippians 4:13. For my son Chase, whose jokes and fun-loving nature fill my life with the unexpected and keep me smiling—1 Corinthians 9:22-27. I love both of you and I am so proud of you, my "Joshuas."

For Phyllis McCoy, an extraordinary fifth-grade teacher, who teaches with her whole heart and loves these kids more than they can imagine. You are such a blessing!—Jeremiah 32:27. (Remember, any old bush will do.)

For Becky Hansard, godly headmaster, who desires every child to know Jesus as Savior and be able to study, understand, and apply God's Word. Press on—Philippians 3:14.

To God be the glory—great things He hath done!

—Janna

CONTENTS

Digging for Truth
A Bible Study *You* Can Do!

DIGGING FOR TRUTH
A BIBLE STUDY YOU CAN DO!

Hey! It's great to see you again. Guess what? Molly and I are going on an archaeological dig, and we want you to come, too! Our Uncle Jake is an archaeologist, and since being an archaeologist is a lot like being a detective, he thought Molly and I would like to spend part of our summer helping him out on a dig. Isn't that exciting? We get to go on a real dig, and Jake says we can bring Sam (the great detective beagle) along, too. Remember how Sam loves to sniff out clues?

While we're on this dig we need to do some crucial research and discover HOW this world began, WHO created the earth, and HOW we got here. These are some very important questions that everyone needs to know the answers to. You'll be able to find the answers to those questions because you have God's Word, the Bible, the source of all truth, and God's Spirit to lead and guide you. You also have this book, which is an inductive Bible study. That word *inductive* means this study will help you investigate the Book of Genesis and discover *for yourself* what it means, instead of depending on what someone else says it means. Isn't that awesome?

So are you ready to become a member of a real archaeological dig team, able to dig out the truth in God's Word? If so, then pack those suitcases and we'll meet you at the site. Here's a list of some things you'll need as we begin our journey to the Fertile Crescent to find out WHEN and HOW it all began.

See you at the site!

THINGS YOU'LL NEED
▼

NEW AMERICAN STANDARD BIBLE
(UPDATED EDITION)—OR PREFERABLY,
THE NEW INDUCTIVE STUDY BIBLE (NISB)
PEN OR PENCIL
COLORED PENCILS
INDEX CARDS
A DICTIONARY
THIS WORKBOOK

1

THE DiG SiTE

GENESiS 1

You're here! Uh-oh—watch out! Here comes Sam, and he is sooooo excited to see you once again.

"Sam, stop that! Get down, Sam! Quit licking their faces! They see you."

Sorry about that. Sam had so much fun working with you in *How to Study Your Bible for Kids* that he is just a little excited. Why don't we head on over to our tent and give Sam a chance to settle down? Uncle Jake and the team have our tent set up, so we can put away our gear. Then we'll be ready to get started on our new adventure in Genesis, Part One.

THE ADVENTURE BEGINS

Hey, you look great in those khakis! The first thing we need to do today is get our instructions from the "site boss." We need to check in with Him the first thing each day before we begin our work. Do you know WHO our "site boss" is? That's right—it's God! Before we can do anything, we need to go to God in prayer and ask Him for His wisdom and guidance so that we will be able to understand the truths that we will dig out in His Word.

So, first things first. Pray and thank God for this great opportunity to spend time with Him digging out His precious truths. Then ask Him for His help. We will never arrive at our destination without God leading us and showing us the way. Now grab those backpacks and let's head over to Site #1.

SITE #1

Now that we are at the site, let's talk about what an archaeologist does. An archaeologist tries to uncover the whole story of how people lived in the past—sort of like a detective who solves the mystery by searching for clues at the crime scene. Archaeologists try to solve the mystery of the past by locating a site. Then they study and research the history and written records that deal with that site. After they finish their research, they carefully plan a dig so they can search for clues to find evidence that shows what really happened in the past. We are going to do the same thing as we study the Book of Genesis. We will study the history and written records (the Bible), then dig out the truths that give us the evidence of WHAT really happened in the beginning and HOW the world came into being.

Since Uncle Jake and the team have already located our dig site, our first job will be to get some pictures of the site before we start to dig. We need to see the big picture of what is happening in the book we are studying by doing an overview of the book. To do an overview, you usually read the entire book that you are studying. Since Genesis is such a long book, in this study we will only read chapters 1–5 to do our overview. The overview will help us understand the author's reason for writing the book, and what the main events are in the book. It will also help us to see the context of the book we are studying.

Context is very important in studying the Bible because it helps us make sure that everything is interpreted correctly. So what is *context?* Context is the setting in which something is found, which is not only important in Bible study but in archaeology also. Context is a combination of two words: *con,* which means "with," and *text,* which means "what is written." So when you look for context in the Bible, you look at the verses surrounding the passage you are studying. Then you also think about where the passage fits in the big picture of the chapter and book you are studying, and then how the passage fits into the whole Bible.

Context also includes:

- The place something happens. (This is geographical context—like the Fertile Crescent and not the United States and Canada.)

- The time in history an event happens. (This is historical context—such as the time before Noah and the flood, or the time after the flood.)

- The customs of a group of people. (This is cultural context—such as people in Bible times lived in tents. For example, Abraham, who was a very rich man, lived in a tent and not a house. They also wore tunics and not blue jeans.

It's always important to be on the lookout for context because it helps you discover what the Bible is saying. We can find context by observation. We begin by looking at the things that are obvious—that's the things that are the easiest to see. In the Bible the three easiest things to see are always:

1. people (WHO?)

2. places (WHERE?)

3. events (WHAT?)

So as we get started today, let's keep our eyes open for the obvious in Genesis 1 by turning to our Observation Worksheets. Observation Worksheets are pages that have the Bible text printed out for you to use as you dig out truth for your-self.

Turn to page 138 and read Genesis 1.

One thing an archaeologist needs on his or her site is an artist to draw any important finds. After you have finished reading Genesis 1, you're going to do the artist's work. Sketch the main event that you uncover in Genesis 1 in the box below.

Now ask yourself, WHAT is happening in this chapter? Then write a title for the main event on the line below the box. A title is a very brief description that tells what the main event is. A title should:

1. be as short as possible

2. describe the main thing the chapter is about

3. if possible, use words you find in the chapter instead of your own words

4. be easy to remember

5. be different from the other titles so that you can tell them apart

Genesis 1

Creation

That was a great discovery! Now before we leave the site today, let's get some practice in decoding hieroglyphics. You never know when we might run across a message written in this ancient Egyptian language. So let's practice our skills by decoding the message below. It's a very important message that tells us why it's important to know God's Word, and how we know we can put our total trust in what the Bible says. Decode the message by using our hieroglyphic code. Find the word in the hieroglyphic code that matches the drawing in our message below. Then write the word that matches the picture on the blanks underneath the code.

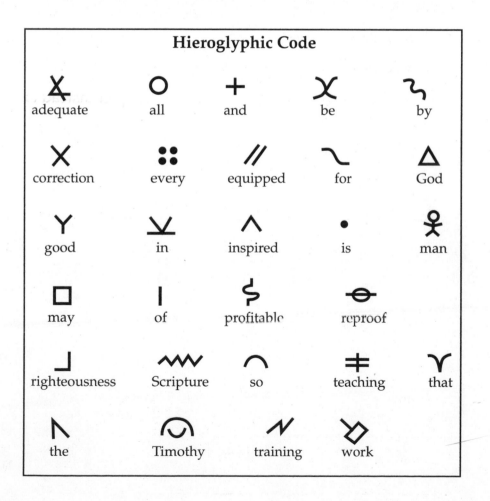

Hieroglyphic Code

adequate	all	and	be	by
correction	every	equipped	for	God
good	in	inspired	is	man
may	of	profitable	reproof	
righteousness	Scripture	so	teaching	that
the	Timothy	training	work	

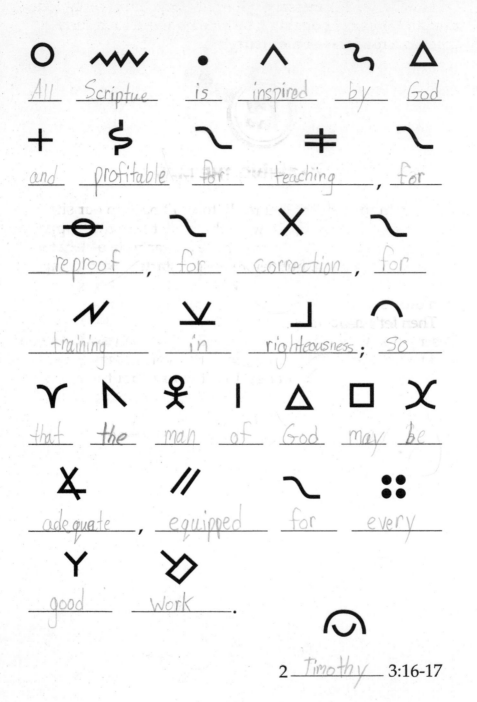

○ 〰 · ∧ ろ △
All Scriptue is inspired by God

＋ ⌇ 〜 ≠ 〜
and profitable for teaching , for

⊖ 〜 ✕ 〜
reproof , for correction , for

Ν ⋎ ⌐ ⌒
training in righteousness ; so

Ψ ↗ ⚲ I △ □ ✕
that the man of God may be

⅄ ∥ 〜 ⠶
adequate , equipped for every

Υ ◇
good work .

⌣

2 _Timothy_ 3:16-17

Now write this message (your memory verse) on an index card and start memorizing it by reading it out loud three times in a row, three times today!

DRAWING THE MAP

Good morning! Are you ready to head back to our site? Today we will continue drawing the main thing that happens in Genesis to help our surveyor have a clear map of what's important in our dig. But before we get started, Sam is yapping. He's trying to make sure we don't forget to check in with our "site boss" first. Have you prayed? Good.

Then let's head to the site by turning to page 141 to our Observation Worksheet on Genesis 2. Read Genesis 2. As you read today, mark every reference to the word *Adam* in a special way by coloring it orange. Don't worry about marking any of the pronouns or synonyms that go with *Adam*. Just mark the word *Adam*.

Now WHERE is the first place that you see the word *Adam?* Give the chapter and verse where *Adam* is used first.

Gen 2:20

Now draw the big picture of what happens in Genesis 2 in the box below and title it for our surveyor.

Genesis 2

The First Woman

Did you notice that both Genesis 1 and 2 deal with the same subject? WHAT is that subject? the C R E A T I O N

Wow! You did it! You have uncovered our first clue in the book of Genesis. Now before we head to the showers, let's practice our memory verse "3 x 3"—that's out loud three times in a row, three times each day.

IN THE FIELD

"Hey, Molly, are you ready to do some more research? I love drawing these archaeological 'maps.' It is so awesome seeing how each chapter fits together."

How about you? Are you ready to head to Genesis 3 and draw the next part of our map? Don't forget to talk to the "site boss" first, then turn to page 144 and read Genesis 3. Mark every reference to the word _Adam_ in a special way by coloring it orange just like you did yesterday.

Now draw the main event and give it a title.

Genesis 3

The Disobedience

Fantastic! Another piece to our map is drawn! Hang in there. You are doing a great job at laying the groundwork. We need a complete archaeological map before we can begin our dig.

CONTINUING THE GROUNDWORK

"Hey, Max, pass the canteen. It's so hot out here."

"It sure is, Molly. Can you believe all the research we've done so far? We are almost ready to begin digging. I can hardly wait!"

"Me, too, Max."

So let's hurry and head back to our Observation Worksheet on page 147. While we have a cool drink we can read Genesis 4. Let's read it and mark every reference to the word *Adam* by coloring it orange just like we did yesterday.

Now sketch the main event in the box below and write a title underneath the picture.

8/25/10

Genesis 4

The First Death

You've got it down. How are you doing on your memory verse? Try saying it to a friend or a grown-up. Sam is so proud. He's wagging his tail!

FINISHING THE MAP

"Can you believe it, Max? We only have one more chapter to do for our overview, then our map will be complete and we'll be ready to start digging."

"I know, Molly. Sam can't wait either. You know how he loves to dig."

So let's grab our pencils and sketch pads and head to Genesis 5 on page 150. Read Genesis 5 and mark *Adam* the same way we have in the other chapters.

Then take a brown pencil and underline the phrase *"and he died."* Each time you see the phrase "and he died," write out beside the phrase how long each man lived, according to what the Bible says.

Now make your sketch on the main event in Genesis 5 and put your title underneath your sketch.

Genesis 5

You did it! You now have the big picture of what happens in the first five chapters in Genesis. Aren't you excited about all you've seen? And we've just begun to scrape the surface.

WHO do you think wrote the Book of Genesis? From your overview you've discovered that Genesis is a book about the beginning, about Creation, so WHO was there to tell how it actually happened except God?

Orthodox Jews and Christians believe that Moses wrote the first five books of the Bible. Do you know the names of the first five books in the Bible? Write them out below:

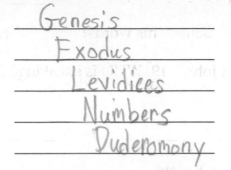

Genesis

Exodus

Levidices

Numbers

Dudenomony

These five books were known as the Torah, or the Pentateuch. (Did you know that *penta*, the first part of the word *Pentateuch*, means "five"?) In fact, when you read in the Bible where the Jews speak about the book of the law, they are talking about these first five books of the Bible, the Torah. Did you know that there are other men who don't believe that Moses wrote the Torah? These men claim the first five books were written by several different authors.

So let's find out for ourselves. Let's check out what the Bible has to say about WHO wrote this very important book of beginnings. Let's compare Scripture with Scripture by going to other passages in the Bible. This is called cross-referencing. Remember, Scripture is the best interpreter of Scripture. As we look at other passages of Scripture, we will see what they say about WHO wrote this book. We have to also remember to keep an eye out for context by looking at the verses that come before the verse we are looking at, and the verses that come after the verse we are looking at.

Look up and read John 5:46-47.

WHO is speaking? WHO is the "Me"? (Hint: Look at verse 19 to discover who the "Me" is.)

Jesus

WHO wrote about Jesus?

_____*Moses*_____

Should we believe his words? ____✓____ Yes _____ No

Now read John 7:19. WHO is speaking? (Hint: Look at verse 16.)

_____*Jesus*_____

WHO gave the law?

_____*Moses*_____

So from looking at these verses, WHO would you say the author of Genesis is?

_____*Moses*_____

But HOW did Moses write Genesis when he wasn't even born until the time of Exodus? HOW did Moses know what to write? Let's go back to the Word and see WHAT the Bible tells us.

Look up and read 2 Peter 1:20-21.

2 Peter 1:21 HOW did men know what to write?

Men __*were moved*__ by the __*Holy*__ __*Spirit*__

spoke from __*God*__.

Read Exodus 17:14. WHAT did God tell Moses to do?

_____

Read Exodus 24:4. WHAT did Moses do?

He built an alter, & set up 12 pillers. (1 for each tribe of Israel)

Now let's review your memory verse, 2 Timothy 3:16-17.

All Scripture is __inspired__ by God.

The Greek word for *inspired* is *theopneustos*. It is pro-nounced like this: theh-op'-nyoo-stos. Why don't you try say-ing it? *Theos* means "God" and *pneo* means "to breathe." So the word *inspired (theopneustos)* means the Scripture is "God-breathed." Isn't that awesome? We know we can trust what the Bible tells us because it comes directly from God.

Yes, ordinary men wrote the books in the Bible. But we see very clearly that God is the One who told the men what to write. These men were moved by God's Spirit to write what He wanted them to say. The Bible doesn't contain God's words; it is the Word of God. It is "God-breathed" and is good for teaching, for reproof (which means to tell someone he is doing something wrong), for correction (which means to bring someone back to the right way), and for training in righteous-ness (which means to give the right instruction and correcting so that someone can be right and have a right relationship with God).

Now that you know HOW the Bible was written and WHERE the words came from, Molly and Max want you to think about these very important questions:

- Do you believe WHAT the Bible says?
  __√__ Yes ____ No

- Will you choose to believe what the Bible says over what man says? __√__ Yes ____ No

- Will you allow God's words to show you where you are wrong? __√__ Yes ____ No

- Are you willing to be corrected? Will you change what's wrong to what's right, even if means changing what you believe? __✓__ Yes ____ No

Great work! Our archaeological map is done, and we have already seen some very important truths that we need to remember and apply to our lives. As we head for our tent, take a moment to think about what you learned that you didn't know before. Thank God for loving you enough to create you and give you His holy Word so that you can know truth and live in a way that pleases Him. Then let's hit the sack. Morning comes early, and tomorrow the dig begins!

2

THE EXCAVATION BEGINS

GENESIS 1

As Max was sleeping he suddenly felt something wet and rough on his face. "Ugh!" he thought as he cracked his eyes open. "What is that? Sam! Stop that, Sam. Quit licking my face! Get down, boy!"

Laughing, Molly glanced at the clock. "Hey, Max, he's just trying to wake you up. It's time for breakfast and then we get to start digging."

"Oh man, I can't believe I forgot that today was the big day. No wonder you were trying to wake me, Sam. The groundwork is almost finished, and the fun is about to begin. I'll race you to the mess tent, Molly!"

Are you ready to join Max and Molly as they start digging out God's truths in Genesis 1? This week we will begin looking at the details in the first chapter of Genesis to find out exactly WHAT happened in the beginning and HOW it happened. So grab your shovels and race Molly, Max, and Sam to the site.

SEARCHING FOR CLUES

"We're here!"

"Shhh, Molly. The area supervisor has the drawings out, and I can't hear everything he's saying."

"Okay, everyone, the survey is complete. Let's drive the stakes into the ground and map out the grid." The area supervisor was just finishing his directions as Uncle Jake approached the site.

"Sorry you didn't get to hear, Max. Here comes Uncle Jake. We'll ask him."

"Hey, Uncle Jake," asked Max, "what does he mean about driving in the stakes and mapping out the grid?"

"Well, Max, in the beginning of an excavation we have to draw a grid system on a topographical map. That's a very detailed map that shows the place or region exactly like it is. This map will help us decide which areas we want to excavate (which means dig out) first. Then we drive stakes into the four corners on the area of ground that we are going to excavate, and stretch string to each stake in order to outline a square. After that, we will divide up the inside of the big square into smaller individual squares that are about five meters by five meters using the string and stakes. Each square will be lettered and numbered like this: A1, A2, etc., and each square will have its own supervisor to keep a daily journal of the excavation work, finds, and observations."

"Wow, I didn't realize how much work you had to do before you ever start to dig, Uncle Jake. Do you think we'll get to break ground today?"

"Not today, but it won't be too long, and it'll be worth the wait. So are you ready to get started?"

"As soon as we pray, we'll be ready to go."

Now help Max and Molly draw the grid by turning to Genesis 1 on page 138 and marking your key words and key phrases.

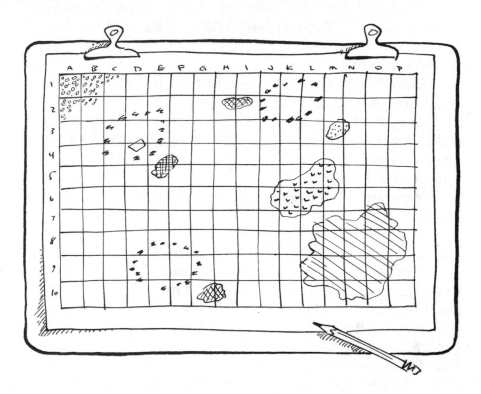

What are *key words?* Key words are words that pop up more than once. They are called key words because they help unlock the meaning of the chapter or book that you are studying and give you clues about what is most important in a passage of Scripture.

- Key words are usually used over and over again.

- Key words are important.

- Key words are used by the writer for a reason.

A key phrase is like a key word, except it is a group of words that are repeated instead of just one word. Such as "I did it," "I did it," "I did it." The group of words "I did it" is a phrase that is repeated instead of just one word.

Once you discover a key word or a key phrase, you need to mark it in a special way using a special color or symbol so that you can immediately spot it in Scripture. You also need to watch and see if there are any pronouns or synonyms that go with the key word or key phrase, and mark them also. What are pronouns and synonyms? Take a look at your maps below.

PRONOUN MAP

Pronouns are words that take the place of nouns. A noun is a person, place, or thing. A pronoun stands in for a noun. Here's an example: "Molly and Max race to the dig site. They can't wait to get started." The word *they* is a pronoun because it takes the place of Molly and Max's names in the second sentence. It is another word we use to refer to Molly and Max.

Watch for these other pronouns:

I	you	he	she
me	yours	him	her
mine		his	hers

we	it
our	its
they	them

MAP ON SYNONYMS

Synonyms are different words that mean the same thing. For example, *sailboat, yacht,* and *rowboat* are different words, but they are all names of kinds of boats. These words are synonyms.

Now that you know what key words, pronouns, and synonyms are, turn to page 138 to your Observation Worksheet on Genesis 1. Read all of Genesis 1 and mark the following key words and key phrases. Also mark anything that tells you WHEN something happened with a clock like this:

God (draw a purple triangle and color it yellow. Don't forget to watch for pronouns.)

There was evening and there was morning, _____ day (circle in green and put a clock over the time like this: This is a key phrase.)

And it was so (double-underline in orange)

after their (its) kind (circle in red)

Great work! Now let's head over to the mess tent. We're hungry. Hey, guess what? Before we eat, Uncle Jake has something to show us in another tent. He wants us to see part of a stone tablet that he uncovered at a different dig. Let's take a look.

Isn't that cool? But we can't quite read the message on the tablet. Some of the letters are worn off. Can you look at the clues below and figure out the message that was once written on this stone tablet? Turn to Genesis 1 and see if you recognize this verse. Then fill in the missing blanks on the tablet below and write this verse on your index card. It will be your memory verse this week.

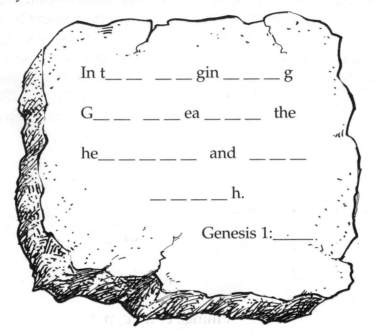

In t__ __ __ __ gin __ __ __ g

G__ __ __ __ ea __ __ __ the

he__ __ __ __ __ __ and __ __ __ __

__ __ __ __ h.

Genesis 1:____

Now practice saying it out loud how many times in a row? _____ And how many times today? _____ Way to go! Let's go eat, and we'll see you back at the site tomorrow.

STUDYING THE GRID

Whew! It's another hot day! Being an archaeologist is a hot and dirty job, but it's also really cool, too, getting to investigate the past.

   One skill that archaeologists and their teams need to be very good at is the skill of observation. They have to examine everything they find very closely. They even examine the soil! We worked on this skill yesterday as we uncovered key words. Today we will look at another way to develop this very important skill.

   As archaeologists study the site, they ask questions. Those questions help them think through how things might have happened. We need to practice this skill of asking questions as we continue to examine Genesis 1. We need to learn how to ask the 5 W's and an H. Do you know what the 5 W's and an H are? They are the WHO, WHAT, WHERE, WHEN, WHY, and HOW questions that help us dig out the truth of what happened in the past.

1. Asking WHO helps you find out:
   WHO wrote this?
   WHOM was it written to?
   WHOM do we read about in this section of Scripture?
   WHO said this or did that?

2. WHAT helps you understand:
   WHAT is the author talking about?
   WHAT are the main things that happen?

3. WHERE helps you learn:
   WHERE did this happen?
   WHERE did they go?
   WHERE was this said?

   When we discover a "where," we double-underline the "where" in green.

4. WHEN tells us about time, and we mark it with a green clock like this:
   WHEN asks questions like:
   WHEN did this event happen? Or WHEN will it happen?
   WHEN did the main characters do something?

It helps us to follow the order of events, which is so important to an archaeologist.

5. WHY asks questions like:
   WHY did he say that?
   WHY did this happen?
   WHY did they go there?

6. HOW lets you figure out things like:
   HOW was this done?
   HOW did people know something had happened?

Now that we know how important it is to ask questions and think things through, let's get started looking at the site. Turn to page 138 to your Observation Worksheet on Genesis 1. Read Genesis 1:1-5 and answer the questions below.

Genesis 1:1 WHO created the heavens and the earth?

_____ GOD _____

Genesis 1:1 WHEN were they created? (Did you put a clock over this?)

_____ In the begining. _____

Genesis 1:2 HOW was the earth described in the beginning?

_____ The earth was formless & void. _____

Genesis 1:2 WHAT was over the surface of the deep?

_____ Darkness _____

Genesis 1:2 WHAT was the Spirit of God doing over the surface of the waters?

_____ moving _____

Genesis 1:3 HOW did light come into the world?

God said, "Let there be light."

Genesis 1:4 WHAT did God see?

the light

Genesis 1:4 WHAT did God do with the light?

He divided the light from darkness.

Genesis 1:5 WHAT did God call?

a. _the light Day_

b. _the darkness Night_

Genesis 1:5 HOW long did this take? WHAT key phrase did you mark in this verse?

_____

Now turn to page 44 and keep a record of your excavation work by listing your finds and observations on the Days of Creation in your daily journal. List WHAT God created on Day One. Then on your Observation Worksheet on page 138 write "Day One" beside Genesis 1:1-5. If you have a *New Inductive Study Bible,* you may want to do this right in the margin of your Bible instead of on your Observation Worksheet.

Now read Genesis 1:6-8 and ask the 5 W's and an H.

Genesis 1:6 WHAT did God bring into existence next?

_____

Genesis 1:6-7 HOW did He bring it into existence?

_____

Genesis 1:6-7 WHAT did the expanse separate?

_____

Genesis 1:8 WHAT did God call the expanse?

_____

Genesis 1:8 HOW long did this take? WHAT key phrase did you mark in this verse?

_____

Now turn to page 44 and write what you uncovered on Day Two by listing WHAT God created in your daily journal. Then on your Observation Worksheet write "Day Two" beside Genesis 1:6-8.

You did a great job examining the evidence today! Before you hit the showers, don't forget to practice your memory verse.

PASSiNG OUT ASSiGNMENTS

"Sam, where are you going, boy?" Max shouted. "Sam! Sam! Come back here!" Max continued to shout Sam's name as Sam skidded to a stop right in front of you, our junior archaeologists in training. Sam ignored Max as he jumped up to give your faces a good licking. "Whoa, Sam! Get down, boy," said Max as he finally caught up with Sam and scooped him into his arms.

As you can tell, Sam is thrilled to have you back at the site once again. Uncle Jake has just handed out our assignment. We're going to continue to examine the evidence in Genesis 1 today by asking the 5 W's and an H questions, and then we're going to find the answers in a word search. So, junior archaeologists, have you spent time with the "site boss" this morning? Good! Then let's get started by turning to our Observation Worksheet on pages 138-139 and reading Genesis 1:9-19.

Now examine the facts and question the text.

Genesis 1:9 WHAT did God do next?

a. _____ the _____ in one place

b. let the _____ appear

Genesis 1:10 WHAT did God call the dry land?

_____

Genesis 1:10 WHAT did God call the gathering of the waters?

_____

Genesis 1:10 WHAT did God see?

_____

Genesis 1:11-12 WHAT did God tell the earth to bring forth?

_____, _____, _____

Genesis 1:12 HOW were they to bring fruit and yield seed? (Hint: It's a key phrase from Day One.)

_____

Genesis 1:12 WHAT did God see?

_____

Genesis 1:13 HOW long did this take? WHAT key phrase did you mark in this verse? "There was_____ and there was _____, a _____."

Genesis 1:14 WHAT did God say next? "Let there be _____ in the _____ of the heavens."

Genesis 1:14-15 God gives six reasons for the lights. List those six reasons.
a. to _____ the _____ from the _____
b. for _____
c. for _____
d. for _____ and
e. for _____
f. for lights in the _____ of the heavens to give _____ on the _____

Genesis 1:16 HOW many great lights did God make? WHAT are they? _____ great lights.
a. the _____ light to govern the day. WHAT is the great light that governs our day? the _____

b. the _____ light to govern the night. WHAT light governs our night? the _____

WHAT other lights did God create also? the _____

Genesis 1:18 WHAT did God see?

_____

Genesis 1:19 HOW long did this take? WHAT key phrase did you mark in this verse? "There was_____ and there was _____,

a _____."

    Now circle the answers from each individual blank in the word search below. If a phrase fits on one blank, then it will run together in the word search like this: ITWASGOOD. If an answer has more than one blank, then you need to find each individual word separately. Some answers may be repeated more than once, but you only need to circle each answer one time in the word search.

D	N	I	K	R	I	E	H	T	R	E	T	F	A	E
M	O	R	N	I	N	G	F	Y	F	H	T	R	A	E
E	I	T	W	A	S	G	O	O	D	R	S	U	x	N
Y	T	Y	G	N	I	N	E	V	E	T	D	I	R	Y
A	A	W	A	E	U	S	E	P	A	R	A	T	E	M
D	T	D	T	S	S	G	S	R	Y	M	L	T	T	U
D	E	A	H	S	Y	N	S	L	N	D	E	R	A	L
R	G	Y	E	T	S	E	A	S	O	N	S	E	E	q
I	E	A	R	H	R	N	A	P	E	S	S	E	R	q
H	V	T	E	G	D	U	L	R	x	R	E	S	G	P
T	C	H	D	I	Y	A	O	T	S	E	R	N	N	R
T	H	G	I	L	N	W	Y	F	A	T	x	G	N	U
x	L	I	S	T	T	F	Y	S	E	A	ß	I	K	O
I	W	N	S	N	O	O	M	J	S	W	q	S	Y	M

Now turn back to page 44 and record your findings by listing WHAT God created on Day Three and Day Four in your daily journal.

Then on your Observation Worksheet or in your Bible write "Day Three" beside Genesis 1:11-13 and write "Day Four" beside Genesis 1:14-19.

Great investigation! Your research is really paying off.

MORE DISCOVERIES

Good morning! The area supervisor has decided to divide up some of the teams today. We're almost ready to dig, and we need to make sure our tools are in order and that we have enough supplies for the week. So listen carefully as Mr. William, our area supervisor, hands out our assignments.

"Okay, Team #1 will go into town for supplies, Team #2 will organize and check the tools we'll need, and Team #3 will finish examining the site so that we can complete our daily journal on the Days of Creation. Now let's all pray before we head out."

"Wow, Max! I'm so glad that we get to be on Team #3. I can't wait to see what God is going to do next."

"Me too, Molly. Let's grab Sam's leash and our canteens and get to the site."

Turn to pages 139-141 to your Observation Worksheet on Genesis 1 and read Genesis 1:20-31, then dig out the facts.

Genesis 1:20-21 WHAT did God create next?

a._____

b._____

Genesis 1:21 HOW were they created? (Hint: It's a key phrase.) _____ _____ _____

Genesis 1:21 WHAT did God see?

_____

Genesis 1:22 WHAT does God do to them?
God _____ them.

Genesis 1:22 WHAT command does God give them?

_____

_____

Genesis 1:23 HOW long did this take? WHAT key phrase did you mark in this verse?

_____

Genesis 1:24-25 WHAT did God create next?

_____

Genesis 1:24-25 HOW did God make them?

after _____ _____

Genesis 1:25 WHAT did God see?

_____

Genesis 1:26 WHAT did God create next?

_____

Genesis 1:26-27 HOW did God make man?
verse 26:

a._____

verse 27: b. m_____ and f_____

Genesis 1:26 WHAT was man to do?

_____

Genesis 1:28 WHAT does God do to them?

God _____ them.

Genesis 1:28 WHAT did God say to them?

a. Be _____ and _____.

b. F_____ the _____.

c. S_____ it.

d. R_____ over the fish, birds, and every
   living thing that moves on earth.

Genesis 1:29 WHAT does God give them?

_____

Genesis 1:31 WHAT did God see?

_____

Genesis 1:31 HOW long did this take? WHAT key phrase did you mark in this verse?

_____

Now read Genesis 2:1-3.

Genesis 2:1 WHAT does this verse say about the heavens and the earth?

They were _____.

Genesis 2:2-3 WHAT does God do on the seventh day?

a. _____

b. _____

c. _____

Now turn to page 44 and record WHAT God created on Day Five and Day Six and WHAT God did on Day Seven in your daily journal on the Days of Creation.

Then on your Observation Worksheet (or in your Bible) write "Day Five" beside Genesis 1:20-23 and write "Day Six" beside Genesis 1:24-31. Then next to Genesis 2:1-3 write "Day Seven." Looking at your daily journal:

• Do you see a design to God's Creation? ___ Yes ___ No

- Did God create the world and the things in it in a logical way? ___ Yes ___ No

- Is there order in God's Creation? ___ Yes ___ No

Isn't that awesome to see that God is a God of logic and order? God didn't create man until He had prepared the earth for man to live in. Plants can't grow without light and water, so God didn't create plants until after He had created both light and water. The living creatures, beasts, and man were not created until there was a place for them to live and food for them to eat. God's Creation shows us what a Master Planner and Designer our God is. Not only is He a God of love and compassion, but He is also a God of logic and order. So as you head back to the tent, why don't you thank God for this amazing Creation that He created from His perfect plan?

Let's Dig

"Max, hurry up. It's almost time to go."

"Oh, Molly, it's barely daylight outside. We have a while before the dig begins."

"I know, Max, but after all we saw about God and His Creation, I thought it would be really neat to have our devotion and prayer time outside as we watch the sun rise this morning."

"Great idea, Molly. Let's go."

As Molly and Max watched the sun come up, Molly sighed. "I just can't get over how God created all of this out of nothing."

"I know, Molly. It's pretty amazing. Oh boy, here comes Uncle Jake now."

As Jake approached the kids, they both had to look up to see their tall uncle's face. "Hey, guys, are you ready? Today is the big day. No more waiting. The digging is about to begin. And since both of you have worked so hard, the team has decided that you should get to dig in the first square."

"Yippeeee! Max, did you hear that?"

"I sure did. Let's race! Come on, Sam."

As Molly and Max raced to the site, they saw the whole team gathered together. Uncle Jake walked up and stood in the middle of them like a basketball coach with his team. "Let's pray first and ask God to bless our efforts and to keep us safe."

When Uncle Jake finished praying, he turned to Max. "Max, grab the shovels, and we're ready to start." As Max returned with the shovels, Uncle Jake finished his directions. "Okay, guys, as we dig up the first layer of soil, we need to put the soil in a bucket. Then we'll empty the buckets of soil into a wheelbarrow and dump them in a special area so that we can examine them later. Now let's get digging! And remember: Be careful with those shovels."

Now it's your turn to help Molly and Max. As you studied the days of Creation, did you notice that God's Creation didn't just happen? There was action on God's part in each part of Creation. So as our dig begins, we want you to excavate the squares that we have marked out on our grid to find the verbs that show our God is a God of action. Do you know what a verb is? Check out our map on verbs below.

MAP ON VERBS

Did you know that every sentence has a verb? A verb is a word that usually shows action. But a verb can also show state of being, it can help another verb, and sometimes a verb will link a word in the predicate to the subject in a sentence.

Let's look at an action verb. An action verb tells what the person or thing in the sentence is doing, such as "Sam digs holes." *Digs* is the action verb in the sentence because it shows what Sam did.

Now let's do some digging of our own by discovering the 12 action verbs of our God by looking at the grid below. To uncover the verbs, use the letter and number pair under each blank. Go to the grid and find the letter, such as A on the right side of the grid, and then go up until you find the number that goes with the A, such as 4. Find the letter in the square that goes with A4 and fill it in the blank. Do the same thing for each blank until you have found all 12 of our action verbs. We've done the first one for you.

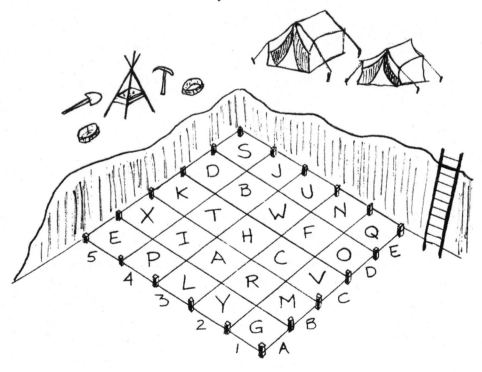

1. God <u>c</u> <u>r</u> <u>e</u> <u>a</u> <u>t</u> <u>e</u> <u>d</u>.
      C2 B2 A5 B3 C4 A5 D5

2. God ___ ___ ___ ___ ___ ___ ___ ___ ___.
     D3 B3 E5   B1 D1 C1 B4 E2 A1

3. God ___ ___ ___ ___.
     E5 B3 B4 D5

4. God ___ ___ ___.
     E5 B3 D3

5. God __ __ __ __ __ __ __ __ __.

    E5 A5 A4 B3 B2 B3 C4 A5 D5

6. God __ __ __ __ __ __.

    C2 B3 A3 A3 A5 D5

7. God __ __ __ __.

    B1 B3 D5 A5

8. God __ __ __ __ __ __.

    A4 A3 B3 C2 A5 D5

9. God __ __ __ __ __ __ __.

    D4 A3 A5 E5 E5 A5 D5

10. God __ __ __ __ __ __ __ __ __.

    C2 D1 B1 A4 A3 A5 C4 A5 D5

11. God __ __ __ __ __ __.

    B2 A5 E5 C4 A5 D5

12. God __ __ __ __ __ __ __ __ __ __.

    E5 B3 E2 C2 C4 B4 D2 B4 A5 D5

Once you have excavated the squares, go back to your Observation Worksheet on pages 138-141 to Genesis 1:1–2:3 and mark these 12 action verbs in a special way on your worksheet by coloring them a color, circling them, or underlining them. Just make sure that you do each verb in a different way or color so it will stand out on your Observation Worksheet.

Next week we'll take a closer look at these verbs that show what God did on each day of Creation. Now sit down and have a cool drink. That was a lot of hard digging you did today, but before you relax too much, find a grown-up or a friend and say your memory verse. What a great way to show other people who created the heavens and the earth!

Daily Journal on the Days of Creation

First Day	Fourth Day
Second Day	Fifth Day
Third Day	Sixth Day
Seventh Day	

3

SHOVELS, PICKS, AND BRUSHES

GENESIS 1

"Hey, Molly, look over here in A4."

"What is it, Max? What do you see?"

"It looks like some pieces of shard—you know, small bits of pottery—and it's mixed in with this layer of soil."

"How awesome, Max, our first find! Let's use the trowels to excavate these shards very gently."

"And we need to mark our grid showing the exact location of our find."

"That's right. I'll call A4's supervisor so she can record this on the excavation log. Then we're ready to examine our find."

A SMALL FIND

Okay, junior archaeologists, let's take a closer look at our find—the action verbs we uncovered last week. Examining them will give us a clearer understanding of what the Bible means.

One way to examine our verbs is to do a word study on them. A word study is where you look at the word in the original language it was written in. Did you know that the Old Testament (where Genesis is found) was written primarily in Hebrew with some Aramaic? So if we want to make sure we understand what the word *created* (one of our action verbs) means in Genesis 1:1, we would do a word study by looking up *created* in a concordance like the *New American Standard Exhaustive Concordance* or Zodhiates's *Complete Word Study Old Testament*, and find out what the word *created* means in the Hebrew language, just like Molly and Max have done in their field notebook.

If you would like to learn how to do a word study on your own, Molly and Max show you how in the *How to Study Your Bible for Kids* book. If you have a copy of this book, and if your mom, dad, or teacher has a *New American Standard Exhaustive Concordance* or Zodhiates's *Complete Word Study Old Testament*, you might want to try and find these words all by yourself.

But just in case you don't, Molly and Max want you to see what they uncovered. Take a look in their field notebook below to see what they found in the word study they did on our action verbs: *created, was moving, said, saw, separated, called, made, placed, blessed, completed, rested,* and *sanctified.* These are the 12 action verbs that show WHAT God did.

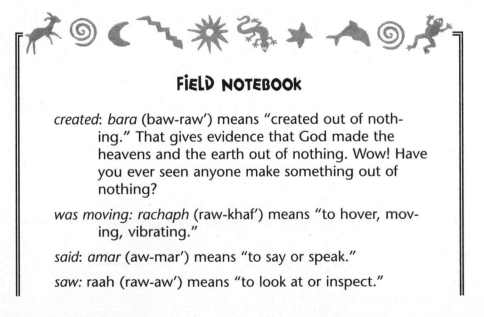

FiELD NOTEBOOK

created: *bara* (baw-raw') means "created out of nothing." That gives evidence that God made the heavens and the earth out of nothing. Wow! Have you ever seen anyone make something out of nothing?

was moving: *rachaph* (raw-khaf') means "to hover, moving, vibrating."

said: *amar* (aw-mar') means "to say or speak."

saw: raah (raw-aw') means "to look at or inspect."

separated: *badal* (baw-dal') means "to divide or distinguish."

called: *qara* (kaw-raw') means "to call out, cry out."

made: *asah* (aw-saw') means "to work, fashion, construct, build."

placed: *nathan* (naw-than') means "to set, commit, put, hang, set forth, putting something in or on a place, or fastening something in place."

completed: *kalah* (kaw-law') means "to accomplish, to bring a process to completion, at an end, finished."

rested: *shabat* or *shabath* or *shavath* (shaw-bath') means "to cease, desist, rest, leave off, to bring to an end."

blessed: *barak* (baw-rak') means "to praise, salute, bend the knee, bow."

sanctified: *qadash* or *qadhash* (kaw-dash') can mean "holy, consecrate, to be set apart, to be clean, or make clean."

Now do a little digging of your own. Turn to your Observation Worksheet on page 138 and take a closer look at how these verbs are used. They should be easy to spot since you marked each one in a special way last week.

How many times do you see "God created?" _____ times

Name the things that God created out of nothing:
Genesis 1:1_____

Genesis 1:21_____

_____

Genesis 1:27_____

Looking at "was moving" in Genesis 1:2, WHO was moving (hovering, vibrating) over the surface of the waters?

_____

HOW many times do you see "God said"? _____ times

Look up and read Psalm 33:6. HOW were the heavens made?

_____

WHAT did God speak into existence?

Genesis 1:3 _____

Genesis 1:6 _____

Genesis 1:9 _____

Genesis 1:11 _____

Genesis 1:14 _____

Genesis 1:20 _____

Genesis 1:24 _____

Genesis 1:26 _____

WHAT is the key phrase that we see in verse 9 that gives us the result of God speaking?_____

Now can you speak and have it happen? ___ Yes ___ No

Look up and read Hebrews 11:3.

a. HOW do we understand that the worlds were

prepared? by _____

b. HOW were the worlds prepared?

by the _____ of _____

By looking at what the words *created* and *said* mean, we see just how powerful God is. He can make something out of nothing. He speaks and it happens. God's Word has power. It is by His Word that the worlds were prepared, and it is by faith that we believe it. We are to take God at His Word and believe what He says.

Do you see how important it is to study and know God's Word? ___ Yes ___ No

Do you live out what God's Word says? Do you obey God? ___ Yes ___ No

Now that you have seen what God spoke into existence, look at two other verses in Genesis where we see God saying something to man.

Genesis 1:28 WHAT does God say to man?

_____

_____

Genesis 1:29 WHAT does God say to man here?

_____

Isn't that impressive to see God both blessing and providing for man's needs?

HOW many times do you see the phrase "God saw"?
_____ times

From looking at what *saw* means in the Hebrew,
WHAT did God look at or inspect? all of His

c __ __ __ __ __ __ __

WHAT is the key phrase in these verses that tells WHAT
God thought about His creation?

_____ _____ _____

Did God make anything bad? _____ Yes _____ No

Did God make any mistakes? _____ Yes _____ No

   That includes you! So don't complain about who you are,
what you have, or how you look. Remember that God created
you and saw that it was good!
   Well, the sun is going down and it's getting cool out here,
so we had better finish this up tomorrow. But before you grab
your jacket and head to the mess tent, Molly and Max need a
little help with the shards of pottery they discovered today.
Help them brush off the dirt. Then look at the broken pieces
and see if you can figure out how they would fit together to
make a whole piece of pottery. We have labeled each piece of

shard with a word. So as you figure out how they should fit together, look at the picture of the whole vase. Try to figure out how the broken pieces would fit on the whole vase. Write the word on the shard piece that matches the piece on the whole vase. Then place them in order on the blanks below. We've done the first one for you.

<u>God</u> _____ _____ _____ _____ _____

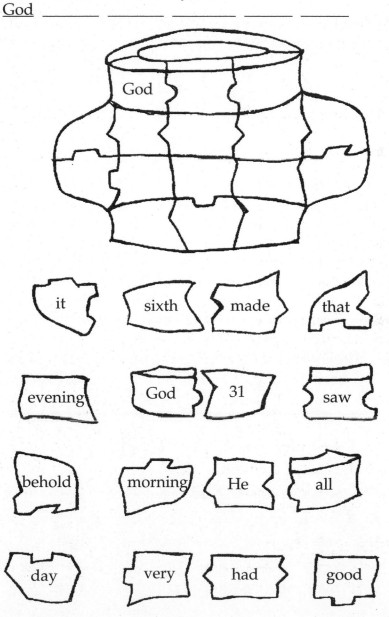

it   sixth   made   that

evening   God   31   saw

behold   morning   He   all

day   very   had   good

_____, and _____, _____ was _____

_____. And there was _____

and there was _____, the _____ _____.

Genesis 1: _____

What a find! You discovered your memory verse for the week. Don't forget to write it out on an index card and say it out loud three times in a row, three times today. Remember: "3x3"!

BACK TO THE PIT

As the sun was setting yesterday, we were still looking at our 12 action verbs and their Hebrew meanings. Today as we climb back into the pit, let's pick up where we left off by turning to our Observation Worksheet on page 138 to Genesis 1. Solve the crossword puzzle by examining our action verbs.

Look at where you marked "God separated."
WHAT two things did God separate (divide or distinguish)?

1. (Across) Genesis 1:4 _____ from darkness

2. (Down) Genesis 1:7 _____ below the expanse from_____ above the expanse

   HOW many times do you see "God called"? ____ times
   WHAT did God call?

3. (Down) Genesis 1:5 God called light _____ and

4. (Across) darkness _____

5. (Across) Genesis 1:8 God called the expanse _____.

6. (Across) Genesis 1:10 God called the dry land _____.

   HOW many times do you see "God made"? ____ times

WHAT did God make (build, construct, or fashion)?

7. (Across) Genesis 1:7 _____

8. (Down) Genesis 1:16 _____ _____ _____

9. (Across) Genesis 1:25 the _____ of the earth

10. (Down) the _____, and everything that creeps on the ground

11. (Down) Genesis 1:26 _____

WHAT did God place (hang or put in its place)?

12. (Down) _____

13. (Down) _____

14. (Across) _____

Now look at Genesis 2:1-3 on page 141.

WHAT did God complete (accomplish, bring to an end, finish)?

15. (Across) the heavens, and the earth, and all their _____

Genesis 2:2 WHAT did God do when He completed His Creation?

16. (Across) He _____ from all His work.

WHY? WHAT does that word mean (look at your field notebook on pages 46-47)?

_____

Was God tired? _____ Yes _____ No

No. God doesn't get tired like we do. This word means He stopped what He was doing. He was finished with His work, so He ceased His work and did two things to the seventh day.

WHAT are those last two verbs? _____
and _____

So after God was finished, He blessed what He had done and made the seventh day holy. He sanctified it (set it apart) from the other six days.

Aren't you amazed at seeing HOW God brought this world into being? Look at all God did each day.

Do we have to guess how it happened, or does God tell us very plainly WHAT He did?

_____

We don't have to guess or wonder because our God, the Master Designer, a God of logic and order, tells us exactly how He brought everything into being. All we have to do is read His Word. AMAZING! Now what do you need to do

before you climb out of the pit? That's right—practice your
verse. You are amazing, too!

Day Three

DiggiNg DEEPER

"Hey, Max, you better get Sam. It looks like he's going a
little crazy."

"Sam, stop that! I know you love to dig, but we have to
take it slow and easy so we can make sure we don't miss anything or destroy a find. Come on, boy. Uncle Jake has a special
test pit for you right over here."

Are you ready to go a little deeper in our study? Have you
p__ __ __ __ __? Then grab a pick as we probe a little deeper
today to see if God created the heavens and earth all by
Himself. Read Genesis 1:26-27 on your Observation
Worksheet on page 140.

   Looking at Genesis 1:26 WHO is the "Us"? Do you have any clues? Let's see what we can discover by taking a look at what the Hebrew word for *God* is in Genesis 1:1 and 1:26-27.

   To find the Hebrew name for God, solve the maze below. Look at the objects on the left side of the column. Now put the first letter of that object in the correct box on the right by following the path from the object to the correct box. Then read down the column on the right from top to bottom to discover what the Hebrew word for *God* is in Genesis 1:1 and 1:26-27.

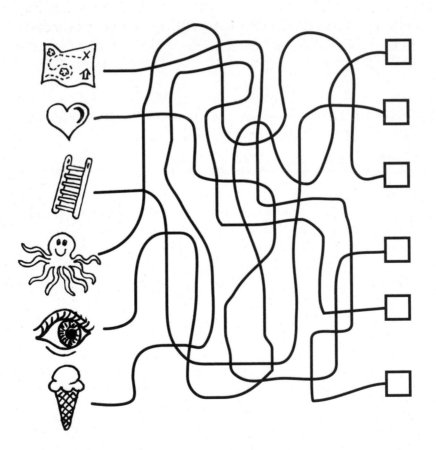

   Now write out this Hebrew word here: _____
   What does this word mean? This word designates God as God. It means "to fear" or "to reverence." The first part of the

word, *El*, means "mighty or strong." It is the word we use to refer to Almighty God. The *im* ending is very important because it is a plural ending. *Elohim* is the word for God as Creator in Genesis 1:1. Since it has a plural ending, does this mean that there is more than one person that has the attributes (qualities) that make God to be God, and different from man? There is only one God who is one in character and attributes. But God is also three distinct Persons: God the Father, God the Son, and God the Holy Spirit. Since we have discovered that *Elohim* is the Hebrew word used for *God* in Genesis 1:1 and that it has a plural ending, could this mean that God the Father, God the Son (Jesus Christ), and God the Holy Spirit each had a part in Creation? HOW do we find out?

First let's look at Genesis 1:2. WHO was moving over the surface of the waters?

_____

Now let's do some cross-referencing. Look up and read John 1:1-3,14.

John 1:1 WHO was in the beginning?_____

John 1:1 WHO was the Word? _____

Let's list what we see about the Word in John 1:1:

a. The Word was in the _____.

b. The Word _____ _____ God.

c. The Word was _____.

Hmmmm. Isn't that interesting? The Word was not only God, but the Word was with God.

So HOW many are claiming to be God? _____

What do you think that means? Could it mean that the Word was not only God, but also someone else? Let's find out.

John 1:2 WHO was in the beginning with God?_____

WHO is this "He"? Read John 1:14. WHO became flesh and dwelt among us, WHO is the only begotten from the Father, and WHO is God's Son?

_____

Look up and read John 10:30. WHAT does Jesus say about Himself and the Father?

_____

Now go back to John 1:3. HOW did all things come into being?

_____

And WHO did we discover was this "Him"?

_____

Look up and read Hebrews 1:2. Through WHOM was the world made?

_____

Look up and read Colossians 1:13-17. WHO is the "He" in these verses?

_____

Now read 1 Corinthians 8:6.

WHAT do we see about God?_____

_____

WHAT do we see about Jesus? _____

_____

So by looking at all these verses, we see that God, Jesus, and the Holy Spirit each had a part in Creation. Now go back to Genesis 1:26-27. Do you know WHO the "Us" is? Name the "Us."

_____

Isn't that awesome to discover for yourself that God, Jesus, and the Holy Spirit each had a part in creating man, and that man was created HOW?

_____

You were created in the image of God—AMAZING!

Aren't you glad that you went a little deeper into God's Word?

Psalm 7:17 says, "I will give thanks to the LORD according to His righteousness and will sing praise to the name of the LORD Most High."

As you climb out of the pit today, praise God for who He is: our Creator and a mighty, awesome God!

READING THE LAYERS

Guess what? Today we get to help Uncle Jake and Hannah, our soil scientist, read the layers of the soil. Doesn't that sound like fun? And while we're at it, we need to investigate another layer in Genesis 1 that has to do with timing. What 5 W's and an H question deals with timing? WHEN. That's right! So today as we get started testing our soil, let's take another look at the WHEN in Genesis 1. Turn to your Observation Worksheet on page 138 and read Genesis 1:1. Or better yet, say it out loud for practice since you already have this verse memorized.

So WHEN did God create the heavens and the earth?

_____

WHEN was the beginning? And HOW old is the earth? Did you know that a lot of scientists and textbooks say the earth is billions of years old? Does that agree with what the Bible says? And if what others say doesn't line up with what the Bible says, WHOM are you going to believe: God or man? WHERE are you going to put your faith?

So let's take the first step to finding our answers. Let's look at Genesis 1:1–2:3 and see what the Bible has to say.

HOW long did it take God to create the earth?

_____

HOW long is a day? When we talk about a day, we mean the time it takes for the earth to turn on its axis one time, which is a 24-hour period of time. Is that what God meant when He used the word _day_ in Genesis? Let's find out.

The Hebrew word for *day* in Genesis is *yom*, which has several meanings. It can mean a period of light as contrasted with darkness, a period of 24 hours, vague time, or a point of time. How do you know which meaning to use? By looking at the context of the passage of Scripture. Do you remember what context is? Context is where we look at the verses that surround the Scripture passage we are studying, like the verses before it and the verses after it. Then we think about how the passage fits into the chapter, and then how it fits into the whole Bible.

So let's take a closer look in Genesis 1 to see what we discover about the word *day* by looking at the context of the passage.

Now WHERE is the first place we see *day* mentioned in Genesis 1? WHAT verse? _____

In the first part of verse 5 we see God calling the light WHAT?

_____

Which does this *day* sound like? Circle the answer you think is correct.

a. a 24-hour period of time

b. a time of light as contrasted with darkness

In the second part of this same verse we see our key phrase *"There was evening and there was morning, one day."* This phrase is repeated five more times (in Genesis 1:8,13,19, 23, and 31).

WHAT do you think *day* means in these verses? Circle the answer you think is correct.

a. a 24-hour period of time

b. a time of light as contrasted to darkness

c. a vague amount of time

WHY did you choose this answer?

_____

_____

_____

In Genesis 2:2 WHAT did God do on the seventh day?

_____

Now let's compare Scripture with Scripture. Look up and read Exodus 20:1-3 to put you in context of what is happening.

In these verses we see God speaking to Moses, giving him the law. Now read Exodus 20:8-11.

Exodus 20:9 HOW long were the children of Israel to work?

_____

Exodus 20:10 WHAT were the children of Israel to do on the seventh day?

_____

Exodus 20:11 WHAT event were the children of Israel to pattern their days after?

_____

Does this sound like our week? HOW many days are in our week?

_____

Do we have a day of rest that we are to honor God on?
____ Yes ____ No

Since God told the children of Israel to pattern their week after the days of Creation, do you think from looking at the context that God created the earth in six days that were 24 hours long?
____ Yes ____ No

WHY or WHY NOT? _____

_____

_____

_____

Look up and read Psalm 33:6-9.

Psalm 33:9 Looking at this verse, does it sound like it took a while for Creation to happen, or did it happen immediately when God spoke?

_____

Now as an example, let's look at an earthly king. When an earthly king issued an order, was it obeyed?
____ Yes ____ No

How fast was it obeyed? Whenever? Immediately? (Circle the correct answer.)

The answer is *immediately*, isn't it? Because someone who didn't immediately follow the orders of his king could get his head cut off! That shows how much power an earthly king had. If an earthly king had that kind of power, think about how much power our God, the Ruler of the universe, has. Is there any reason to believe that the moment when God spoke, it wouldn't have happened immediately? Of course not! Our God is God Almighty, and NOTHING is ever too hard or too difficult for Him!

Now by looking at the context of these verses, we have discovered for ourselves just how God used the word *day*. We know that *day* is used in the first part of verse 5 as a time of light and not darkness. And in the second part of verse 5, along with verses 8,13,19,23, and 31, we see that *day* is a 24-hour period of time. Isn't it awesome being able to understand the Bible for yourself so no one can ever lead you astray?

Now that we know how long it took God to create the earth (that is, if we are going to believe the Bible), tomorrow we will see if we can discover just how old the earth really is.

You did a great job reading the different layers of our soil! So take a break and take Sam for a run. Oh, and don't forget to practice your verse. See you in the morning.

A BiG FiND!

"Molly, get over here! Look—what's that?"

"I don't know, Max. Let's get Uncle Jake or Mr. William to take a look before we do anything."

"Hey, Uncle Jake, we think we found something. Will you please take a look?"

"Sure, Max. Let me get Mr. William and we'll be right over."

"Okay, guys. What's up?"

"Look, Uncle Jake. What do you think it is?"

"Hmmmm, I'm not quite sure, Max, but we need to be very careful to use a small pick and brush to expose it. It looks like part of a bone. It could be a skeleton. So let's leave it *in situ*—that means to leave it in its original place, just like we found it. Mr. William, call Mary Frances over here to get some photographs. Great work, kids!"

Isn't that exciting? Molly and Max may have uncovered something really big. Now it's your turn. One of the biggest questions ever asked is, "How old is the earth?" There are all kinds of books, magazine articles, and scientists doing research to find the answer to this very important question. And because you know where to go to find truth (the Bible), you have the perfect map to dig up the answer to one of the biggest questions ever asked. So are you ready to make history with the world's greatest find? Then pick up that pick and brush and let's expose the truth.

Molly and Max have made a time line on page 69 to help us see how long it's been since God created the earth. We know from what we have studied that God, Jesus, and the

Holy Spirit were before the beginning, in eternity, and that time did not begin until Genesis 1:1, "in the beginning." This is when God created time.

After God creates time, He creates the heavens (space) and the earth (matter). God is the originator of time, space, and matter—the very beginning of the universe.

So since we have seen that time begins with the creation of the heavens and the earth, Molly and Max have placed Creation as the very first event on our time line at 0 years.

Now to find out how old the earth is, we need to trace what happened from Creation until now. Let's start with the creation of man (Adam) on the sixth day and trace all of Adam's generations. Do you remember reading Adam's generations in Genesis 5? Go back to page 150 and read Genesis 5:1-3.

Genesis 5:3 HOW old was Adam when he had Seth?

_____

Now look on the chart below. We put Adam's age when he became the father of Seth in the last column. Now read each verse listed on your chart. Fill in the age of each father that tells when he fathered the son that is listed in the third column.

Verse	Father	Son	Age of Father
Genesis 5:3	Adam	Seth	130
Genesis 5:6	Seth	Enosh	
Genesis 5:9	Enosh	Kenan	
Genesis 5:12	Kenan	Mahalalel	
Genesis 5:15	Mahalalel	Jared	
Genesis 5:18	Jared	Enoch	
Genesis 5:21	Enoch	Methuselah	
Genesis 5:25	Methuselah	Lamech	
Genesis 5:28	Lamech	Noah	
Genesis 5:32	Noah	Shem, Ham, Japheth	
Genesis 11:10	Shem	Arpachshad	
		Total	

After you have listed all of the ages, add them together and put the total number of years in the last column beside the word *Total*.

Read Genesis 11:10. HOW many years after the flood was it when Shem had Arpachshad? _____ years after the flood

Now take the total number of years on your chart and place it in the first blank below. Next put how many years it was after the flood that Shem had Arpachshad in the second blank and subtract it to get the number of years from Creation (Adam) until the flood.

_____ (Total years) - _____ (years after the flood when Shem had Arpachshad) = _____ years from Creation until the flood.

Go to your time line on page 69 and put your answer in the blank under "The Flood" on your time line.

Now look at the second chart below and read each verse that is listed. Fill in the ages just like you did on the first chart. This chart takes you from Arpachshad to Abram (Abram's name was later changed by God to Abraham—Genesis 17:5).

Verse	Father	Son	Age of Father
Genesis 11:12	Arpachshad	Shelah	
Genesis 11:14	Shelah	Eber	
Genesis 11:16	Eber	Peleg	
Genesis 11:18	Peleg	Reu	
Genesis 11:20	Reu	Serug	
Genesis 11:22	Serug	Nahor	
Genesis 11:24	Nahor	Terah	
Genesis 11:26	Terah	Abram, Nahor, Haran	
		Total	

Now add up the number of years and put it in your Total column on the chart. Then take this number and put it on your time line on page 69 in the blank under Abraham's name. This covers the time period from the flood up to Abraham.

Look up and read Matthew 1:17. Fill in the next chart below by reading Matthew 1:17 and putting how many generations there were from Abraham to David. Do the same thing for the generations from David to the deportation to Babylon and from the deportation to Babylon to the Messiah (Jesus Christ). Let's add up how many generations there were from Abraham to Messiah (Jesus), placing the total number of generations on the chart.

Verse	Events	Number of Generations
Matthew 1:17	Abraham to David	
	David to Deportation to Babylon	
	Deportation to Babylon to Messiah	
	Total	

So how much time do you think a generation might be? A generation is an average time period between the birth of the parents and the birth of their children. So a generation was probably somewhere between 30 to 50 years. The Bible doesn't tell us exactly how long a generation is, so we have to estimate (make a guess) how long we think a generation would be.

Let's say a generation is around 30 years. Take the number of generations that you just added up on your chart and multiply it by 30. Like this:

_____ (total number of generations) x 30 (total number of years in a generation) = _____ years

Now try making a generation around 50 years. Take the number of generations that you just added up on your chart and multiply it by 50.

_____ (total number of generations) x 50 (total number of years in a generation) = _____ years

This shows you approximately the number of years from Abraham to Messiah. *Approximately* means "almost exact, to come close to." This means that this number of years is very close to the correct number of years from Abraham to Messiah (Jesus), but it is not the exact number of years. We don't know the exact number because we don't know exactly how long a generation really was. So take the two answers that you got from making a generation 30 years and 50 years and place each of these answers on your time line in the blanks under "Jesus." Put the answer for 30 years in blank A and the answer for 50 years in blank B. This is the approximate number of years from Abraham until Jesus.

Looking at our time line, we see there is only one blank left, and that's the "Now" blank, which is the year you are living in right now. The calendar that we use today is based approximately on the time of Jesus' birth: 4 B.C. So we can place the year that we are living in right now (for example, 2001) on our time line in the blank under "Now."

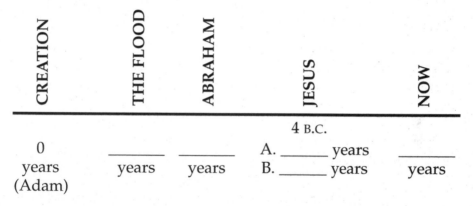

Now to find out how old the earth is, look at your time line and add up all the years that you wrote in the blanks from Creation until now. When you get to the blank for Jesus, use the number of years in blank A under "Jesus" on your time line.

The beginning of time, 0 years, Creation (Adam) + _____ years Flood + _____ years Abraham + A. _____ years Jesus + _____ years Now = _____ years, the approximate age of the earth.

Now do this one more time using the numbers in blank B under "Jesus" on the time line.

The beginning of time, 0 years, Creation (Adam) + _____ years Flood + _____ years Abraham + B. _____ years Jesus + _____ years Now = _____ years, the approximate age of the earth.

WHAT is range of the total number of years of the earth? Put the lowest number of years that you totaled in the first blank below and the highest total in the second blank

from _____ years to _____ years

The reason we did a range of the total numbers of years is because we had to estimate (make a guess) on how long a generation was. But even though we do not know exactly how old the earth is, we can come very close by looking at what the Bible says.

Is the earth billions of years old? ____ Yes ___ No
How about millions of years? ____ Yes ___ No
But books and some scientists say that the earth is billions or millions of years old. Are they wrong? HOW do you know?

_____

So WHOM are you going to believe: God, our Creator, or man whom God created and who is limited in his knowledge and experience?

_____

Wow! You did it! You just made the biggest discovery in all of history! The earth is not millions or billions of years old. It is only thousands of years old! We are so proud of all your hard work this week. You kept digging away, and just look at what you have uncovered—a very big find! Now spread the news. Show someone else this very amazing discovery!

4

EXTRACTING THE EVIDENCE

GENESiS 1

Molly and Max are really excited about their discovery last week. As we continue with our dig, Uncle Jake is consulting with a physical anthropologist named Dr. Murphree. So what is a physical anthropologist? That's someone who studies the physical characteristics of human beings. A physical anthropologist identifies human remains, which is usually their bones.

Today as Dr. Murphree examines and extracts the evidence, she needs to confirm what Max's find is. We will continue to extract evidence on how God created the earth. Let's get started. The team is waiting for us so that we can spend some time together with our "site boss." Then it's back to work!

iDENTiFYiNG EACH LAYER

In order to identify each day of Creation in greater detail, we need to look at one layer at a time. As we uncover each

73

layer, we need to help our site artist sketch these layers so that we can record our find.

So let's begin by reading the first part of Genesis 1:2:

> The earth was formless and void, and darkness was over the surface of the deep.

WHAT does it mean to be "formless and void"? Check out Molly and Max's field notebook below.

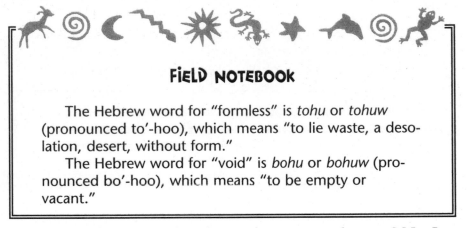

FIELD NOTEBOOK

The Hebrew word for "formless" is *tohu* or *tohuw* (pronounced to'-hoo), which means "to lie waste, a desolation, desert, without form."

The Hebrew word for "void" is *bohu* or *bohuw* (pronounced bo'-hoo), which means "to be empty or vacant."

So does that mean that the earth was a total waste? No. It just means that God had not given it a form or a shape. It was empty because He had not put anything on it yet. As we have seen from looking at Genesis 1, God spends the first four days of Creation giving the earth and the heavens their shape, and then He populates it.

> So WHAT do you think the earth might have been like from looking at the description in Genesis 1:2?

_____

> Find another clue to what the world was like by looking up and reading 2 Peter 3:5.

> WHAT do you think the earth might be like from this verse?

_____

Does water have a form? _____ Yes _____ No

To see for yourself, pour some water into different-shaped containers. Does the water keep the same shape in each container, or does it change its shape depending on the shape of the container?

_____

Now draw a picture in the box below to show HOW the earth looked when it was formless and void, and darkness was over the surface of the deep.

Look at the next layer by reading the second part of

```
┌─────────────────────────────────────────────┐
│                                             │
│                                             │
│                                             │
│                                             │
│                                             │
│                                             │
│                                             │
│                                             │
└─────────────────────────────────────────────┘
```

Genesis 1:2:

> And the Spirit of God was moving over the surface of the waters.

Do you remember our Hebrew word for "was moving"? Go back and look at what it means again in Molly and Max's field notebook on page 46. Then draw God's Spirit (you could draw a dove or the symbol we use when we mark the Holy Spirit as a key word, like this: Holy Spirit colored yellow and drawn in purple). Show God's Spirit hovering, moving, and vibrating over the surface of the waters.

We have already seen that God created time, space, and matter. Now this vibrating of the Holy Spirit could be the beginning of energy in our universe since vibration is in itself energy.

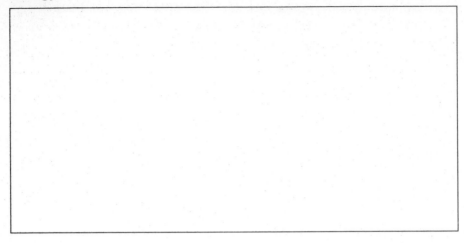

Read Genesis 1:3:

"Then God said, 'Let there be light'; and there was light."

Before you draw this light, read Genesis 1:14-18 on your Observation Worksheet on page 139. WHAT does God create on the fourth day?

s_____, m_____, and s_____

Since God doesn't create the sun, moon, and stars until Day Four, WHAT is this light on Day One?

Look up and read Revelation 21:1-2,23-25.

The context of this verse is when God creates the new heaven and the new earth after Jesus comes back the second time.

Does the city (the New Jerusalem) need the sun or moon to shine upon it? _____ Yes _____ No

WHY or WHY NOT? _____

_____

So WHERE does light come from on Day One?

That's right—it comes from God because God is the source of light. Now draw a picture of Genesis 1:3: "Then God said, 'Let there be light'; and there was light."

Now draw Genesis 1:4: "God saw that the light was good; and God separated the light from the darkness."

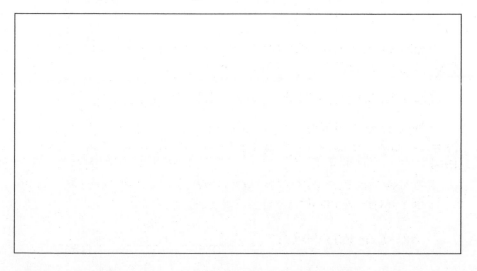

You did a great a job drawing all the different layers in the first day of Creation! Now before you race Molly and Max back to the campsite, practice your math skills to uncover this week's memory verse. Archaeologists need good math skills to help them measure their site, to know how far and how wide to dig, and to make sure their records are accurate.

So sharpen those math skills. Uncover your Bible verse by looking at the clues underneath the blanks below your research card. Each blank has a math problem underneath it. Work each problem and find the answer on your research card. Write the letter that goes with the correct answer on your card on the blank. For example, if the math problem is 5x7, look at your research card and find 35, the correct answer to the math problem 5x7. Then write the letter that goes with 35, which is the letter T, on the blank that has 5x7 underneath it.

RESEARCH CARD

A=6	B=8	C=10	D=12	E=14	F=16	G=18
H=9	I=15	J=21	K=24	L=27	M=20	N=28
O=36	P=44	Q=48	R=25	S=30	T=35	U=40
V=45	W=50	X =55	Y=60	Z=49		

___ ___ ___ ___   ___ ___   ___ ___ ___   ___ ___ ___
5x7 5+4 3x5 40-10 7+8 5x6 7x5 6+3 24-10 2x6 3+3 5x12

___ ___ ___ ___ ___   ___ ___ ___   ___ ___ ___ ___
5x10 10-1 3x5 5+5 3x3 5x7 8+1 16-2 24+3 4x9 5x5 7+5

___ ___ ___   ___ ___ ___ ___   ___ ___ ___   ___ ___
12-3 4+2 5x6 10+10 2x3 8+4 28-14 3x9 2x7 5x7 20+20 5x6

___ ___ ___ ___ ___ ___ ___   ___ ___ ___   ___ ___
5x5 10+4 3x7 40-4 3x5 7+3 2x7 5+1 4x7 2x6 10-2 2x7

___ ___ ___ ___   ___ ___   ___ ___.
9+9 3x9 7-1 10+2 3x5 4x7 10+5 5x7

___ ___ ___ ___ ___ 118:24
4x11 15+15 8-2 3x9 4x5

Now let's race! First one to the campsite gets the first s'more!

SKETCHING OUR FIND

"Mmmmmm! Those s'mores sure were good last night!"

"I liked them too, Max! I am so glad Uncle Jake invited us on this dig. I never realized how many details there were in God's Creation until we started uncovering it one layer at a time. I can't wait to expose the next layer."

How about you? Are you ready to grab those colored pencils and sketch pads and start sketching Day Two? Great! Then let's head to our Observation Worksheet on pages 138-139 and read Genesis 1:6-20. Mark each place you find the key word *expanse* on your Observation Worksheet by coloring it blue and drawing a purple circle around it like this: (expanse) (remember to watch for pronouns).

Genesis 1:6 WHERE is the expanse?

Genesis 1:6-7 WHAT does the expanse separate?

_____

Genesis 1:8 WHAT does God call the expanse?

_____

Now draw Genesis 1:6-7:

> Then God said, "Let there be an expanse in the
> midst of the waters, and let it separate the
> waters from the waters." God made the expanse,
> and separated the waters which were below the
> expanse from the waters which were above the

> expanse; and it was so.
> "God called the expanse heaven. And there was evening
and there was morning, a second day."

You're becoming quite an artist! Don't forget your memory
verse. See you tomorrow.

MORE DIGGING!

"Hey, guys! How is it coming?"

"Great, Uncle Jake. No wonder you love being an archaeologist."

"I thought I would stop by and work with you on the next layer. By the way, where's Sam? I haven't seen him lately."

"He's over there taking a nap. I think all this digging has worn him out."

"Well, let's get to work while Sam is still asleep."

Turn to page 138 to your Observation Worksheet on Genesis 1. We need to dig out some key words. Read Genesis 1 and mark the following key words:

waters   dry land

seas (color it blue)   earth (color it brown)

seed (color it green)

Now get out your field notebook and make a list, recording what you learn about each of these key words, along with the phrase you marked in Week Two: *after their (its) kind.*

FIELD NOTEBOOK

Waters:

Genesis 1:2 The _____ of _____ was
_____over   the surface of the waters.

Genesis 1:6-7 Let there be an _____ in
the midst of the waters, and let it _____
the waters above from the waters below.

Genesis 1:9 Let the waters below the _____
be _____ into _____ _____.

Genesis 1:10 The gathering of the waters God called
_____.

Genesis 1:20 Let the waters _____ with
_____ of _____ _____.

Genesis 1:22 _____ the waters in the seas.

Seas:

Genesis 1:10 God called the _____ of the
_____, seas.

Dry Land:

Genesis 1:9 God said, "Let the waters...be gathered
_____ _____ _____."

Genesis 1:10 God called the dry land _____.

Earth:

Genesis 1:1 God created the _____.

Genesis 1:2 The earth was _____ and
_____.

Genesis 1:11 The earth sprouts _____,
_____ yielding seed, and _____
_____ after their kind.

Genesis 1:20 Let _____ _____ above
the earth.

Genesis 1:22 Let _____ _____ on the
earth.

Genesis 1:24 Let the earth bring forth:
a. _____ _____ after their kind
b. _____
c. _____ _____
d. _____ of the earth after their kind

Genesis 1:26 _____ is to rule over all the earth.

Genesis 1:28 Man is to _____ the earth and
_____ it, and _____ over it.

Seed:
Genesis 1:11-12 The earth brought forth
_____: _____ yielding
seed, and _____ _____ bearing _____
with seed in them, _____ _____ _____.

After Their Kind:

Genesis 1:11-12 God made _____ _____ bearing _____ after their kind.

Genesis 1:12 God made _____ yielding _____ after their kind.

Genesis 1:21 God created the great _____ _____ and _____ _____ _____ that moves, with which the _____ swarmed after their kind, and every _____ _____ after its kind.

Genesis 1:24-25 God made living _____ after their kind: _____ and _____ _____ and _____ of the _____ after their kind.

Great digging! Tomorrow we will use our field notebooks as we do our sketches for the third day of Creation. Now as you head for the mess tent, practice your verse with Molly and Max. Why don't you sing it out loud to the Lord?

NEW SKETCHES

Up and at 'em! Another day is here, so it's back to the drawing board once again. Now as we get ready to sketch our find, look at Genesis 1:9-10:

> Then God said, 'Let the waters below the heavens be gathered into one place, and let the dry land appear'; and it was so. God called the dry land earth, and the

gathering of the waters He called seas; and God saw that it was good.

Are all of the seas we have today in one place, or are there many different seas in many different places?

_____

Today we have many seas in many places, but when God first created the earth they were all in one place. Did you know that before you studied Genesis? We will find out more about this in Genesis, Part Two. But do you remember a major event that begins in Genesis 7 that could have changed the earth? Write it out: the _____

Now sketch Genesis 1:9-10 in the box.

Have you ever been to the beach and watched the tides go in and out? Who but God could have orchestrated the wonderful seas and the changing of the tides?

Read Genesis 1:12 on the next page and sketch it out: "The earth brought forth vegetation, plants yielding seed after their kind, and trees bearing fruit with seed in them, after their kind; and God saw that it was good."

Isn't that awesome? Why don't you take a walk outside in your yard, neighborhood, or park and look at all the different trees, flowers, and plants that God made, and experience God's creation for yourself.

Ask your mom or a grown-up for some flower seeds. Plant those seeds in a pot with some dirt, give them some water, and place them in a sunny window. Then watch as those seeds send green shoots up from the soil, grow, and finally blossom.

Or you could ask for a tomato plant so that not only will you get to see it grow and blossom, but you will also get to pick a ripe, juicy tomato—the fruit—off God's plant. What a perfect example of the order of God's Creation. God didn't create the plants until He created the light that plants need to grow, and the earth for them to grow in. He also brought forth the plants with seeds in them so more plants could grow. Isn't our God an amazing God?

EXPOSING ANOTHER LAYER

"Hey, Molly! Guess what? Since this is our last day to work this week, Uncle Jake is going to take us into town this afternoon."

"Yippeee—I can't wait! But boy, our summer sure is flying by."

"It sure is, but what an adventure! Look at all we've learned so far. We have made some great discoveries!"

"Let's see what we uncover next! Come on, Sam. Uh-oh, where's Sam?"

"There he is over by the tent sniffing out clues. We had better hurry!"

Join Molly and Max as Sam leads us in our next adventure in Day Four of God's Creation. Sam has sniffed out the clues we need. So keep your eyes open to discover God's purpose for this day of Creation. To follow Sam's first clue, read Genesis 1:14-19 on page 139. Mark the key word *lights* on your Observation Worksheet by coloring it yellow along with any pronouns and synonyms that go with it.

Do you remember from Week Two WHY God created these lights? Let's list the six reasons that God gave us the lights:

1. _____

2. _____

3. _____

4. _____

5. _____

6. _____

WHAT is the name of the great light that governs the day?

_____

WHAT is the great light that governs the night?

_____

WHAT are the other lights that He made also?

_____

WHERE are these lights?

_____

HOW did they get there?

_____

Can't you just see God placing each star in its exact place? HOW many stars do you think there are?

_____

God placed each one where He wanted it to go. Isn't that amazing?

Read Psalm 19:1. WHAT are the heavens for?

_____

Let's read Psalm 147:4. WHAT does God do?

_____

We see God created all the wonders in the heavens to tell of His glory.

Should we ever look at our horoscope, ask psychics, or study the stars for direction in our lives? Let's see what the Bible has to say about this. Look up and read Deuteronomy 4:19.

WHAT warning does God give in this verse?

_____

Read Deuteronomy 17:2-7.
WHAT happened to the person who worshiped and served the sun, moon, stars, and heavenly hosts?

_____

God had a purpose in creating the lights, but it wasn't for man to worship and serve them. We are not to worship what God has created. We are only to worship our Creator. God's creation was to tell of His glory to point us to Him, the Creator, who alone is worthy of our worship and praise.

So be careful and watch out for those things that take your attention away from God, such as reading a horoscope or calling psychics for help. Remember the consequences in Deuteronomy 17:5. We are to seek God, not His creation, for direction in our lives.

Now read Genesis 1:14-18 again and draw this marvelous creation.

Then God said, "Let there be lights in the expanse of the heavens to separate the day from the night, and let them be for signs and for seasons and for days and years; and let them be for lights in the expanse of the heavens to give light on the earth"; and it was so. God made the two great lights, the greater light to govern the day, and the lesser light to govern the night; He made the stars also. God placed them in the expanse of the heavens to give light on the earth, and to govern the day and the night, and to separate the light from the darkness; and God saw that it was good.

"There was evening and there was morning, a fourth day."

Now take a walk outside. Is the sun shining? Look at how warm and bright it is when the sun is shining. Have you ever seen the sun go behind the clouds and noticed the difference in warmth and brightness when the sun is hidden behind the clouds, and then how it changes once the clouds pass by?

Tonight when it gets dark, go outside and look up at the moon and the stars. God named each one of those stars. Can you count how many there are? If you have a telescope, take a closer look at the moon and stars. If you have a planetarium or an observatory where you live, ask your mom or dad if they can take you to visit it sometime. Or you could go to the library and get a book with color pictures to give you a closer look at God's amazing creation!

But whether you take a walk, read a book, or visit a planetarium, remember why God created these lights: to separate the day from night, to give light on the earth, for seasons, days, and years, and for signs to show us God's glory! So thank God for these wonderful lights that show us just how awesome He is!

Now did you learn your memory verse this week? Sing it out loud, then head to the Jeep. Uncle Jake is going to take Max, Molly, and Sam into the city for more supplies and ice cream to celebrate a job well done.

5

CONTINUING OUR EXPEDITION

GENESIS 1

That was a great trip into town! But now it's time to get back to work. Ben (our site artist) needs for us to get the drawings on the days of Creation finished this week. These drawings have really helped us to see all the details in each day of Creation. How about you? Now we know why an archaeological dig has an artist. It's so the archaeologists can capture the details of each find as they discover it. So let's get started. Let's meet the dig teams for prayer, and then we're headed back to Genesis 1.

SKETCHING THE NEXT LAYER

Let's head over to our Observation Worksheet on pages 139-140 and read Genesis 1:20-22. Before we make our sketch, let's see what God has to say about this fifth day of Creation.

WHAT does God create in the waters?

HOW are they created? What is the key phrase?

_____

WHAT does God create in the open expanse of the heavens, and HOW are they created?

_____

WHAT did God say to them when He blessed them?

_____

Look up and read 1 Corinthians 15:38-39.

Is all flesh the same? _____Yes _____ No

    Do you know what God means by the key phrase *after their kind?* This means God made each plant, water creature, and bird able to have more plants, water creatures, and birds just like itself. Have you ever seen a bird with a fish for a baby? Of course not! God made birds with the genes necessary to have more birds, not fishes.

    You may have learned about these genes in school. Genes are made up of DNA molecules. WHAT is DNA? Take a look at Max and Molly's field notebook.

Deoxyribonucleic Acid

Did you know that every living thing—including plants, animals, and human beings—is made up of cells?

There are 75 trillion cells in the body of an average human being. And each individual cell has as many as 200 trillion groups of atoms called protein molecules.

The largest molecule in a cell is the DNA molecule, which is a short name for deoxyribonucleic (de-ok' se-ri-bo-nu-kle'ik) acid.

WHY is DNA important? Because DNA is the reason all living things can only reproduce after their kind. The DNA molecule carries all the information needed to build plants, animals, or human beings. And all living things get their DNA from their parents.

DNA does not determine only whether a living thing is a plant, an animal, or a human being. It also decides whether you are a boy or a girl, what color your eyes are, your skin color, your height and build, and any other physical characteristics that come from your parents.

DNA never changes, even in the division of a cell.

So by looking at DNA, we can see what a Master Designer our God is. Only God has the intelligence to create something as complex as DNA, which makes each living thing able to reproduce after its kind. Whether it is a plant, water creature, or bird, the parents give their DNA to their offspring. DNA makes it impossible for a bird to give its baby the genes to be a fish, since it does not carry the genes to be a fish. It can only pass on genes to make another bird.

Now read Genesis 1:21-23 and sketch it out.

God created the great sea monsters and every living creature that moves, with which the waters swarmed after their kind, and every winged bird after its kind;

and God saw that it was good. God blessed them, saying, "Be fruitful and multiply, and fill the waters in the seas, and let birds multiply on the earth."

"There was evening and there was morning, a fifth day."

Taking a closer look at God's creation of water creatures will be a little harder since you can't just walk out your back door to take a look at them unless you live at the ocean. But you can visit an aquarium if there is one in your city. Or if you don't have an aquarium, you could get a book from the library and read about all the different ocean zones and how God made each sea creature to fit the zone it lives in by how He made its body, how it finds food, and how it protects itself from its enemies.

Birds will be a lot easier to observe. Make a bird feeder. Take a pinecone and coat it with peanut butter and roll it in birdseed. Glue a piece of yarn or string to the top and hang it outside near a window so you can watch the birds as they eat. Or build a simple birdhouse and watch the birds make a nest, lay their eggs, and have their babies (but don't expect them to have any baby fish). There are so many different ways to watch God's creation in action.

Now before we head to the mess tent, we need to uncover our memory verse for the week. Find the correct path in the maze below by following the arrows that go through all the words in the verse.

Start   God →created →man → image →female
      ↓   ↑   ↑   ↑   ↑

created → man → in → of ← and
   ↓   ↑   ↓   ↑   ↑

male ← own ← His ← God → male
  ↓   ↓   ↑   ↑   ↑

and → image ← God ← of → God
  ↓   ↓   ↑   ↑   ↓

female ← in → the → image ← He
   ↓   ↓   ↑   ↑   ↓

He ← and ← male ← him ← created
 ↓   ↑   ↓   ↑   ↓

created← female ← and → image ← them
  ↑   ↓   ↓   ↑   ↓

image → He → created ← God ← Genesis
  ↑   ↓   ↑   ↑   ↓

them← created →them →Genesis → 2
  ↓   ↓   ↓   ↓   ↑

27 ← 1 ← Genesis ← 1 → 27   Finish

Write this verse on an index card and practice saying it out loud three times in a row, three times each day!

LOOKING FOR CLUES

"Hey, guys," said Uncle Jake as he approached Molly and Max. "I saw your drawings on the fifth day of Creation. I loved those sea creatures and birds. What are you working on today?"

"Nothing yet," Molly replied. "We need to uncover some more information first."

So let's get started. Read Genesis 1:24-26 on page 140 of your Observation Worksheets.

> Then God said, "Let the earth bring forth living creatures after their kind: cattle and creeping things and beasts of the earth after their kind"; and it was so. God made the beasts of the earth after their kind, and the cattle after their kind, and everything that creeps on the ground after its kind; and God saw that it was good.

WHAT does God create and HOW?

_____

Draw this creation.

Now choose a way to watch God's creation in action. Visit a zoo and look at all the different animals that God has created. Or go outside and look for creeping things like a worm, a caterpillar, or a snail. Pet a dog or a cat. Isn't it amazing how God made animals to fit their unique environment (such as polar bears having nice, thick white fur to keep them warm and to help them blend into their surroundings)?

Now let's head to the campfire. Uncle Jake is going to let us have a wienie roast tonight. Before we start roasting those wienies, we need to do one more thing. Can you guess what it is? That's right—we need to practice our memory verse. So let's get to it! Those hot dogs smell pretty good!

THE FINAL SKETCHES

"Hey, Molly, do you think all archaeologists have wienie roasts and s'mores on a dig?"

"I don't think so, Max. I think Uncle Jake planned these cookouts just for us."

"Isn't that neat how Uncle Jake makes everything special for us? He takes such good care of us. Look at how he provides everything we need, and look at all the time he's spending with us to teach us about being an archaeologist."

"Hey, Max, that sounds a lot like God. He takes care of us by providing our every need. He shows us in His Word WHO He is and HOW we can have a relationship with Him. God wants us to be part of His family. He wants us to ask Him for His help in every part of our life. He wants us to have a relationship with Him. Just like we're spending time with Uncle Jake so we can get to know him better, God wants us to spend time getting to know Him."

How about you? Do you know God? Do you have a relationship with Him? Today as we head back to Genesis 1, we will see just how special man is to God as we uncover the last part of Day Six in Creation. So don't forget to pray. Then turn to your Observation Worksheet on pages 140-141, and read Genesis 1:26-31. Mark the key word *man* and any pronouns that go with *man* by coloring it orange.

Now let's make a list for our field notebook on everything we see about man.

FIELD NOTEBOOK

Man:

Genesis 1:26-27 God said, "Let _____ _____ man."

Man is made in _____ _____, in His likeness.

Man is to _____ over the fish of the sea and over birds, the cattle, and every creeping thing on the earth.

Genesis 1:28 God _____ man. God said to man, "Be _____ and _____, and _____ the earth." _____ it, and _____ over the fish, birds, and every living thing that moves on the earth.

Genesis 1:29 God said, "I have given you every _____ yielding seed…and every _____ which has fruit yielding seed; it shall be _____ for you."

Now sketch out Genesis 1:26-27:

Then God said, "Let Us make man in Our image, according to Our likeness; and let them rule over the fish of the sea and over the birds of the sky and over the cattle and over all the earth, and over every creeping thing that creeps on the earth." God created

man in His own image, in the image of God He created him; male and female He created them.

"There was evening and there was morning, the sixth day."

Now read Genesis 2:1 and draw our final sketch.

Thus the heavens and the earth were completed, and all
their hosts.

Show how the earth looked once God's Creation was complete.

"By the seventh day God completed His work which
He had done, and He rested on the seventh day from
all His work which He had done."

You did it! You completed all the sketches for our dig on
each day of Creation! We are so proud of you! Now go grab a
tall, cool glass of lemonade and relax in the shade.

A SPECiAL ASSiGNMENT

"Hey, guys, what are you doing?"
Molly answered Uncle Jake, "Just getting ready to head
over to the site for our next assignment."
"Before you do, I have a special assignment for you. You
have been working so hard studying, mapping out the site,
digging, uncovering the evidence, and drawing our sketches,
that I want you to take some time today to think through all
that you've discovered so far."
"What do you mean, Uncle Jake?" asked Max.
"Well, I know both of you have heard different ideas in
school about how this earth and everything in it came into
being. Have you noticed that the evidence we have uncovered
goes against some of man's ideas?"
"Yes, we were just talking about that last night, weren't
we, Max?"
"Good," replied Uncle Jake, "I'm glad you're thinking and
comparing notes. Why don't we get started on this special
assignment?"
Let's spend the next two days sifting through what man
says could have happened and compare it to what God says
happened. Just because something is printed in a science
book doesn't mean it is a fact. True science does not contradict
what the Bible says. A lot of ideas that scientists have about

the dating of the earth's surface and how the earth came about are not stated facts, but instead they are only theories.

A theory is an assumption, a prediction, a guess about what happened. Do we have to guess what happened in the beginning, or does God tell us in His Word? If we don't believe that what God tells us so clearly in Genesis 1 is true, then how can we believe anything else in His Word? Remember our first memory verse, 2 Timothy 3:16-17: "All Scripture is inspired by God"; it is "God-breathed," which means it comes directly from God to man. So if we can't trust what God's Word says, can we trust God? We have to decide whom we are going to believe: an almighty, all-powerful God, or man who makes mistakes.

Before we look at how some scientists think the earth came into being, and how they date the earth, remember that not all scientists believe the same thing. There are many Christian scientists who believe this world came into being just like God said it did in Genesis 1. There are also many scientists who didn't believe in God, but as they studied science they realized this universe could only have been created by an almighty God, and they became Christians.

Now we know that not all scientists believe the same thing, so let's look at how some scientists who do not believe that God created the earth think the earth came into being.

People who believe that the earth happened over a period of time, that it was just chance and acts of nature that brought it into being, are called *naturalists*. Naturalists believe in evolution. Evolution is a theory (a prediction, a guess) that the earth and everything in it came into being by chance or accident.

One of the evolutionists' theories is the big bang theory. The big bang theory says that all of the matter in the universe was crammed together in a hot, spinning ball of energy that exploded. The pieces flew off and became the galaxies, sun, moon, and stars.

Have you ever seen an explosion on TV or in a movie?
___ Yes ___ No

Did order or disorder come from the explosion? _____

Does it make sense that our beautiful, ordered earth would be created from an explosion? Does an explosion create or destroy?

Not only do some scientists believe the earth came into being by a big bang, they also think the earth couldn't have been created in six days like the Bible says because of the earth's geology.

Geology is a study of the earth's origin, history, and structure. Scientists look at the canyons, mountains, volcanoes, waterfalls, and caves and think that an enormous amount of time had to go by in order for these wonders to have been formed.

But people who believe the Bible remember that a major event happened in Genesis 7 (the flood), which was such a severe catastrophe that it had a major effect on the earth's geology and could have caused canyons and waterfalls to form very quickly.

Scientists also study the fossils that are found. They use different methods to figure out how old a fossil could be. Did you know scientists have dated some fossils to be millions of years old? Is that possible from what we have learned in the Bible?

One method scientists use to figure out how old a fossil could be is called carbon-14 dating. WHAT is carbon-14 dating, and is it reliable? Check out Molly and Max's field notebook.

CARBON-14

When sunlight or starlight strikes the atmosphere, it produces radioactive carbon called carbon-14 (C-14). These radioactive carbon atoms grab onto an oxygen molecule and become carbon dioxide. Plants take in carbon dioxide, which has this radioactive carbon (C-14) in it. Then animals eat the plants. When we eat plants and animals, we get a little bit of this radioactive carbon in our bodies.

When a plant or animal dies, it quits taking in new C-14, and whatever C-14 it has in it begins to decay. About half of it decays in about 5736 years. The time it takes for half an amount of a radioactive element to decay is its half-life. So if you find a fossil and test how much carbon it has, and it has only half as much as the original fossil had, you would say that it was 5736 years old.

Because there is so little of the radioactive element left after ten half-lives or so (5736 x 10 = 57,360 years), C-14 can only date the things that are younger than 60,000 years. It cannot determine something to be millions of years old since it cannot date back more than thousands of years.

Carbon dating also supposes that the C-14 concentrations in the atmosphere have always been what they are today. But this may not be true since the atmosphere changed after the flood (we'll learn about the flood in Genesis, Part Two). We don't really know how much C-14 was in the atmosphere before the flood.

These problems with carbon dating show us it is not a totally reliable method to use in dating animals, plants, and fossils.

Evolutionists also think that once the earth was created from the big bang, then over millions of years a single cell of nonliving matter was changed until it developed into things like fish, birds, and animals. They believe that man evolved (developed gradually) from a single-celled creature until it developed into an animal with a brain, eyes, ears, and nose.

HOW did God tell us in Genesis 1:26-27 that He made man? From an ape? No way! Man is created HOW?

_____

Remember what we learned last week about the phrase "after their kind" and DNA? Is it possible for a bird to have a fish baby?
___ Yes ___ No

No! There are two unchangeable laws of biology on this earth. Life can only come from life, and like always comes from like. A bird is a bird and can only have baby birds, just like a dog can only have more dogs. Has anyone ever seen a bird having a baby fish? Is this a proven fact or just a theory? A theory is just a guess and not true science. Every time a person has a human baby and an animal has a baby just like itself, science proves that like gives birth to like, just as God said, "after its kind"!

Does the theory of evolution make sense? No. Then why do people believe in evolution? One reason is because they have been deceived, just as Eve was deceived in Genesis 3. Satan does not want us to believe in an almighty God who created the heavens and the earth and who is all-powerful. Satan wants us to believe that we are like gods ourselves. This is the basis of New Age thinking: There isn't a difference between the Creator and the creature. Turn to page 144 to your Observation Worksheet on Genesis 3. WHAT did Satan say to Eve in Genesis 3:5 would happen to her the day she ate from the fruit?

_____

So since the beginning of Creation, Satan has set out to deceive man and to make him think that he can be like God. And man's very sin nature wants him to do his own thing, his own way. Man wants to rule, not submit to a holy God.

Let's look up and read Romans 1:18-32.

Romans 1:18 HOW does God feel about men who suppress the truth?

_____

Romans 1:19-20 HOW does God make the truth evident to man?
through **C** __ __ __ __ __ __ **N**

Romans 1:20 Does God show us clearly who He is in creation? WHAT do we see about God by looking at what He made?
His _____ _____ and
_____ nature

Romans 1:20 Do we have an excuse if we do not believe God?
____ Yes   ____ No

Romans 1:21-22 WHAT happens if we do not honor God or give thanks to Him?

_____

Romans 1:25 They exchanged the truth for WHAT?

_____

Romans 1:25 WHOM did they worship?

_____

So if you believe man's theory of evolution, you have exchanged the truth for WHAT? _____ and are worshiping the _____ instead of the

_____

As we head to our tents, let's think about all we've discovered today. Do you believe what the world has to say about how this earth came into being, or do you believe God? Tomorrow we will look at more Scripture verses that give us evidence as to how this world came into being. Don't forget to practice your memory verse, and then lights out! We have another big day tomorrow.

MORE EVIDENCE

"Hey, Molly, what did you think about all we saw yesterday on man's ideas of how the earth came to be?"

"I think it's so sad, Max, that so many people would believe man's word instead of God's Word. I am so glad that Uncle Jake showed us how easy it is to be deceived if we don't discover and know the truth for ourselves. Let's run over to the site. Uncle Jake said he would have more Scripture for us to investigate so we can see for ourselves what God's Word has to say about Creation."

"Okay, I'll race you."

Join Molly and Max as they look up the Scriptures that Uncle Jake gave them. As you read each Scripture, help Molly and Max make a list in their field notebook below on what they find out about God. Start by reading Job 12:7-10 and then listing what you see about God in your field notebook below. Do the same thing for each of the following Scriptures:

Jeremiah 32:17-27

Isaiah 40:21-28

Isaiah 45:11-12

Isaiah 51:12-13

Isaiah 66:1-2

FIELD NOTEBOOK

God:

Job 12:9 The _____ of the Lord _____ _____ this.

Job 12:10 In His hand is the _____ of _____ _____ _____, and the _____ of all mankind.

Jeremiah 32:17 God made the _____ and the _____ by His _____ _____ and by His _____ arm. _____ is too _____ for God.

Isaiah 40:22 God _____ above the _____ of the _____ and _____ out the heavens like a curtain.

Isaiah 40:26 God created the _____ and calls them by _____.

Isaiah 40:28 God is the _____ God, the _____, the _____ of the ends of the earth. He does not become _____ or _____.

Isaiah 45:11 The Lord is the _____ _____ of Israel, and his _____.

Isaiah 45:12 It is I who _____ the _____ and _____ man upon it. I _____ out the heavens with _____ _____ and I _____ all their host.

Isaiah 51:13 The Lord your _____ stretched out the heavens and _____ the _____ of the _____.

Isaiah 66:2 For My _____ _____ all these things.

Now from all the evidence that you have gathered in God's Word, is it clear WHO the Maker, the Creator of the heavens and earth and all that is in them is?

Yes! God shows us very clearly that He is the Creator. We see His glory in all that He created and made. The big question is, Will we believe what God's Word says is truth, or will we try to figure out things for ourselves and be deceived by a lie?

You have dug up the evidence in Genesis and in other passages of Scripture. Does what you believe line up with God's Word? _____ Yes _____ No

If it doesn't, are you going to change your beliefs to God's? Will you allow His Word to train you in His righteousness? This means to let Scripture give the right instruction and correct you so you can be right and have a right relationship with God. Or will you choose to do things your way?

Write out WHAT you are going to do.

_____

As you leave the site today, say your memory verse to a grown-up and share with him or her the wonderful discoveries that you have made about God. Then thank Him for making you in His image.

6

SIFTING THE SOIL

GENESIS 2

"Wow, Max! That was so awesome seeing how Scripture shows us over and over again just who made the heavens and earth and all that is in it!"

"It sure is, Molly, and there are so many more Scriptures we could look up. All we have to do is to keep studying God's Word because God wants us to know Him and His plan for us."

"I can't wait! Uncle Jake said for us to meet him at the pit where we dumped the soil we dug up. I wonder what he's going to teach us next?"

"I don't know, but let's put Sam on his leash and go find out."

BECOMING SIFTSMEN

"Hey, Sam! Where are you, boy? Come here, Sam! Come on, boy! Good dog. Let's go find Uncle Jake at the dirt pit. Whoa, Sam, slow down. What's got into you?"

"I know why he's going crazy, Max. You said dirt pit, and you know how Sam loves dirt."

"Oh no! Help me, Molly, before Sam leaves the camp in shambles."

Why don't you head over to the dirt pit and let Uncle Jake know that Molly, Max, and Sam are on their way. Uh-oh! Here they come now. Grab Sam's leash and let's slow him down!

Good work! Now we're ready to pray, and then Uncle Jake will give us our new assignment.

Uncle Jake is going to teach us how to become siftsmen this week. A siftsman is someone who sifts the dirt from the pit to make sure no tiny objects that might be hard to see are missed. To sift the dirt we need a screen. We will pour the dirt that we've collected on the screen, and then shake the screen gently back and forth to cause the dirt to sift through the small holes in the screen. Any small objects that we may have missed will be caught on the screen while the dirt is passing through the holes. Doesn't that sound like fun?

Let's get busy and read Genesis 1:24–2:25 on pages 140-144. According to Genesis 1:24-31, WHAT is created on the sixth day?

_____

_____

Genesis 1:26-27 HOW is man created?

_____

Let's look in our field notebook below to see what it means to be made in God's image and likeness.

FiELD NOTEBOOK

The Hebrew word for *image* is *tselem* (pronounced tseh'-lem). It means "likeness, resemblance, not an exact duplicate."

The Hebrew word for *likeness* is *demuth* (pronounced dem-ooth'). It means "likeness or similitude." It is a word of comparison.

Isn't that amazing how God made us to resemble Him? Being made in His likeness makes us different from all of His other creations.

Look at Genesis 1:26. WHAT are the things man was to rule over?

a. _____

b. _____

c. _____

d. _____

e. _____

In Genesis 2:1-3 we see the heavens and the earth were WHAT?

_____

Genesis 2:2-3 WHAT did God do on the seventh day?

_____

From reading Genesis 2:4-25, WHAT is God doing?

_____

Since we saw that God finished His creation in Genesis 1:1–2:3, is this a different Creation account in Genesis 2:4-25? NO! Genesis 1 is giving us an overview, the big picture of God creating man, and in Genesis 2:4-25 we see God filling in the details of His Creation.

So let's read Genesis 2 once again and mark the following key words in a special way:

God (Lord God—draw a purple triangle and color it yellow)

earth (color it brown)   tree

garden   man (color it orange)

woman (color it pink)

Good work! Before we leave the dirt pit, let's sift out our new memory verse. Looking at your screen below, you need to sift through all of the words that are a kind of earth: *sand, clay, mud,* and *silt.* As you sift the soil, cross out each one of these words on your screen.

Next cross out all of the names of rocks that you find: *sandstone, shale, slate, granite,* and *marble.* After you get rid of the rocks, sift out all of the minerals by crossing out *graphite, flint, mica,* and *gypsum.* Once the minerals are crossed out, sift out all the crystals by crossing out *quartz* and *salt.* Now write the words that remain on your screen in the blanks below.

For	You	quartz	sand	formed
my	mica	slate	inward	parts
gypsum	You	wove	clay	me
in	my	salt	mother's	mud
silt	womb	flint	I	sandstone
will	shale	give	graphite	thanks
marble	to	mud	You	granite
for	I	silt	quartz	am
fearfully	gypsum	and	wonderfully	clay
salt	made	wonderful	mica	are
shale	Your	marble	works	slate
and	clay	my	sand	soul
mica	knows	granite	it	flint
graphite	very	sandstone	well	silt
sand	Psalm	139:	salt	13-14

_____ _____ _____ _____ _____ _____;

_____ _____ _____ _____ _____ _____

_____.

__ _____ _____ _____ _____ __ _____

_____ __ ____ _ _____ _____ _____

_____ _____; _____

_____ _____ _____ _____, _____ _____ _____

_____ _____ _____ ____ _____ _____.

Psalm 139:13-14

This is your new memory verse, so practice saying it out loud three times—morning, noon, and night—every day!

RECORDING OUR FIND

"Molly, don't forget your field notebook," said Max as he zipped up his backpack. "We're going to record our findings today."

"I've got it right here, Max. Let's see: canteens, flashlights, pencils, notebooks, and journals. Is there anything else we need?"

"I think that's everything except Sam. Now where did he go?"

As Molly and Max started searching the camp, Uncle Jake walked up with a panting Sam. "Sam had a little adventure with a bird as I was inspecting the site this morning. Why don't you take him and head over to the *d-i-r-t p-i-t.*"

"I like the way you spelled out *dirt pit,* Uncle Jake," whispered Max. "Are you afraid Sam will have another running frenzy if you say it?"

"You better believe it. And one running frenzy a day is about all I can handle," laughed Uncle Jake. "See you guys at the pit."

"Let's go, Max," laughed Molly, "before Sam gets into any more trouble."

Now as we head back to the dirt pit, turn to page 141 of your Observation Worksheets and read Genesis 2 again. Then pull out those field notebooks and record what you found by sifting the soil in Genesis 2. Make a list of what you discovered about God and man in your notebook below.

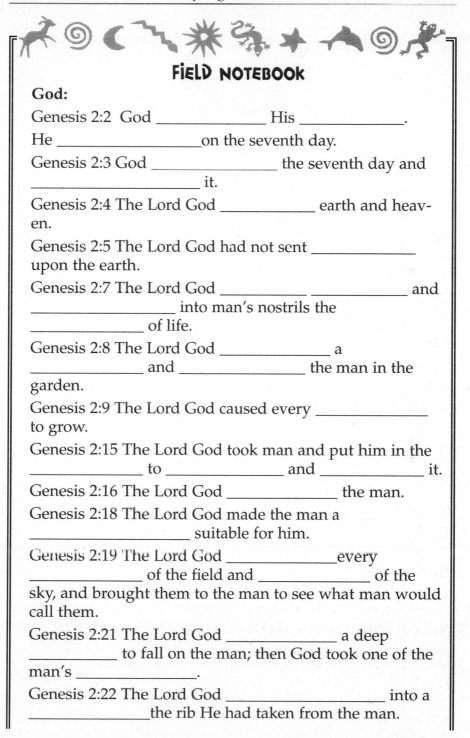

FiELD NOTEBOOK

God:

Genesis 2:2 God _____ His _____.

He _____on the seventh day.

Genesis 2:3 God _____ the seventh day and
_____ it.

Genesis 2:4 The Lord God _____ earth and heaven.

Genesis 2:5 The Lord God had not sent _____
upon the earth.

Genesis 2:7 The Lord God _____ _____ and
_____ into man's nostrils the
_____ of life.

Genesis 2:8 The Lord God _____ a
_____ and _____ the man in the
garden.

Genesis 2:9 The Lord God caused every _____
to grow.

Genesis 2:15 The Lord God took man and put him in the
_____ to _____ and _____ it.

Genesis 2:16 The Lord God _____ the man.

Genesis 2:18 The Lord God made the man a
_____ suitable for him.

Genesis 2:19 The Lord God _____every
_____ of the field and _____ of the
sky, and brought them to the man to see what man would
call them.

Genesis 2:21 The Lord God _____ a deep
_____ to fall on the man; then God took one of the
man's _____.

Genesis 2:22 The Lord God _____ into a
_____the rib He had taken from the man.

Man:

Genesis 2:7 God _____ man from _____ of the _____ and _____ into his nostrils the _____ of _____; and man became a _____ _____.

Genesis 2:8,15 God _____ the man in the _____ to _____ it and _____ it.

Genesis 2:16 God _____ man.

Genesis 2:18 God made a _____ for man.

Genesis 2:19 God brought the beasts and birds to the man for the man to _____ them.

Genesis 2:22 Woman is fashioned from man's _____.

Genesis 2:23 The man calls his helper _____, because she was taken out of man.

Genesis 2:24 A man shall _____ his father and mother, and be _____ to his wife; and they shall become _____ flesh.

Genesis 2:25 The man and his wife were both _____ and not ashamed.

Now head for the campfire and we'll record the rest of our findings tomorrow!

NEW DISCOVERIES

"Hey, Max, I really like being a siftsman."
"Me, too, Molly, and look at Sam rolling around in the dirt.

Sam, oh boy! You are going to have to have a *b-a-t-h* tonight."

As Molly and Max continue to sift the dirt, why don't you record their findings on the earth, the garden, and the tree in the field notebook below?

FiELD NOTEBOOK

Earth:

Genesis 2:1 The heavens and the earth were _____ and all their hosts.

Genesis 2:4 God _____ earth and heaven.

Genesis 2:5 No _____ of the field was on the earth, for the Lord God had not yet sent _____ on the earth.

Genesis 2:6 A _____ used to rise from the earth and water the whole surface of the _____.

Garden:

Genesis 2:8 God _____ the garden toward the _____, in _____; and there He placed the man.

Genesis 2:9 In the midst of the garden was the _____ of _____ and the _____ of the _____ of _____ and _____.

Genesis 2:10 A _____ flowed out of _____ to _____ the garden.

Genesis 2:15 Man was to _____ and _____ the garden of Eden.

Genesis 2:16-17 Man could _____ from any _____ in the garden except for the tree of the knowledge of good and evil.

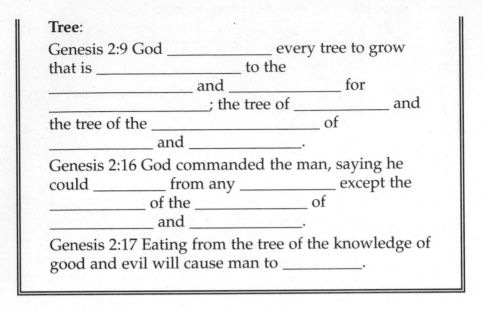

Tree:

Genesis 2:9 God _____ every tree to grow
that is _____ to the
_____ and _____ for
_____; the tree of _____ and
the tree of the _____ of
_____ and _____.

Genesis 2:16 God commanded the man, saying he
could _____ from any _____ except the
_____ of the _____ of
_____ and _____.

Genesis 2:17 Eating from the tree of the knowledge of
good and evil will cause man to _____.

Now climb out of the dirt pit and practice your memory
verse as you help Molly and Max give Sam his *b-a-t-h*. (You
have to spell it out because Sam hates baths.)

RECONSTRUCTiNG THE SCENE

Now that Sam is clean and we have sifted through the soil
and recorded our findings, let's begin to reconstruct the scene
as God tells us more about what happened on Day Six of
Creation.

Before we look for the answers to these 5 W's and an H
questions, did you remember to check in with the "site boss"?
Good job.

Let's reconstruct the scene. Read Genesis 2 on page 141.

Genesis 2:7 HOW did God make man?

God _____ man of _____ from the ground.

God _____into his nostrils, and man became a

_____ _____.

Genesis 2:8 WHERE did God put man to live?

_____

Genesis 2:15 WHAT was man's job?

_____

Genesis 1:29 and 2:16 WHERE was man to get his food?

_____

Genesis 2:16 WHAT was the only thing God told man he could not do?

_____

Genesis 2:17 WHAT would happen if man disobeyed?

_____

Genesis 2:19 WHAT does God get man to do?

_____

Genesis 2:20 After the man names the cattle, birds, and beasts, WHAT does Adam realize?

_____

Genesis 2:21-22 So WHAT does God do next?

_____

Genesis 2:22 HOW did God make woman?

_____

Genesis 2:23-24 WHAT was man and woman's relationship like? WHAT were they to do?_____

_____

Since Genesis 2:24 is talking about marriage, does this
verse help us understand why divorce is wrong? Look
up and read Matthew 19:3-9.

Matthew 19:6 WHY shouldn't a man and woman separate?

_____

Do these verses show you how important marriage is to
God?
____ Yes ____ No

   Isn't it awesome to see how God had a perfect plan for
man? God created man in His image to rule over all creation.
God provided man with a perfect job in a perfect environment, and with plenty of food. God also made the perfect
companion for man so he would not be alone. God made
woman to be a helper to man. He created marriage as a very
special relationship for a man and a woman to share—a relationship that takes two people and makes them one.
   Now as you head to the mess tent, think about all that you
have learned about God and His relationship with man.

A SIGNIFICANT FIND

"Hey, Molly, can you believe this is our last day on our dig? Mom, Daddy, Aunt Kathy, and Uncle Kyle will be arriving tomorrow afternoon."

"I know, Max. I can't wait to see everybody, but it's not really our last day on the dig, because we get to come back in a few weeks."

"I can't wait! We had better fill up our canteens and head back to the pit."

Yesterday as we reconstructed the scene in Genesis 2, we uncovered just how special man is to God. Today as we finish up at the site, let's dig for more evidence that shows WHAT God thinks about man by looking at some cross-references.

Let's read Job 10:8-9. WHAT did God make man out of?

_____

Look up and read Job 33:4. HOW does man have life?

_____

Psalm 100:3 WHO made us?

_____

Psalm 139:13 HOW does God make us?

_____

Isaiah 43:7 WHY were we made?

_____

Isaiah 64:8 WHO is the potter?

_____

WHO is the clay? _____

So should the clay tell the potter how to make the pot?
_____ Yes _____ No

Then why do we try and tell God what we want instead of asking Him what He wants? Will you let God mold you and make you to be more like Him?
_____ Yes _____ No

Go back to Isaiah 43:7 and look at WHY we were created.

WHAT does it mean to be created for God's glory? That means we should live to bring God honor. We should do the things that God wants us to do.

WHAT do you do that brings honor to God? List several things.

_____

_____

_____

Do you do anything that doesn't honor Him, such as telling a lie or making fun of someone at school?
_____ Yes _____ No

Now that you know that God made you to honor Him, does it matter what you do, how you dress, and the language that you use?

____ Yes ____ No

Do you need to treat other people better?

____ Yes ____ No

Do you need to change the way you dress?

____ Yes ____ No

Do you need to clean up your language?

____ Yes ____ No

HOW should you treat other people that God made in His image?

_____

Kids can be so mean to each other, making fun of how big someone's nose is, whether someone is fat or skinny, too smart or dumb. How do you think God feels about kids making fun of each other?

_____

If you make fun of other kids, are you making fun of God's creation? ____ Yes ____ No

God made man very special, unlike any other part of His creation. Say your memory verse out loud. You are fearfully and wonderfully made—you are special! God formed you in your mother's womb to be exactly like you are.

Exodus 4:11 says, "The Lord said to [Moses], 'Who has made man's mouth? Or who makes him mute or deaf, or seeing or blind? Is it not I, the LORD?' "

Does God make mistakes? Absolutely not! We are made in God's image, and we are to bring Him honor. He provided all that we needed from the very beginning of our creation. He blessed us and saw all that He had made, and it was very good.

Think of HOW God made you special. For example, are you good in math, do you like to make up stories, can you sing, are you good at sports, or would you rather play the piano? Write a thank-you note to God below, telling Him how thankful you are for the way He made you and for the gifts and abilities that He has given you:

_____

_____

_____

_____

One way we can honor God is to be nice to everyone and to not make fun of those He created. Why don't you write another note on a piece of paper to someone who is different than you? Encourage him or her by sharing how God made that person special. Tell how you admire the way he can shoot a basketball, or how funny her jokes are. Then put this note in a book or in a locker to surprise the person. What a wonderful way to honor the God that made him or her special, too!

Now as we wrap up Genesis, Part One, we see that God had a plan for the universe. Do you think that God has a plan for you?
____ Yes ____ No

Will you ask God what that plan is and live your life for Him, since you were made by Him and for His glory?
____ Yes ____ No

You did it! You have just dug up God's truths in Genesis, Part One. We are sooooooo proud of you! Now let's head to the campsite to show off our significant finds!

BACK AT THE CAMPSITE

Wow! Can you believe that our dig is finished? It seems like only yesterday we pulled into camp and changed into our khakis and headed to the site. Look at all we discovered. We know WHO made the earth and *about* HOW old the earth is. We have seen that God the Father, God the Son (Jesus), and the Holy Spirit all had a part in Creation. We saw that God is a God of action, that He is a God of order and logic, and that He had a perfect plan for each part of His creation. We know, no matter what anyone tells us, that we are created in God's image. We are fearfully and wonderfully made. That is so awesome! Our God is so AMAZING! He is a Master Designer who created a perfect earth for you and me.

Is the earth a perfect place today? We'll find the answer to that question as we continue to dig up truth in Genesis, Part Two, *Digging Up the Past.* Aren't you excited that our expedition isn't really over? Will you come back and help us discover WHAT happens in the garden after God creates the first marriage? It's sure to be one very exciting adventure. Oh, and don't forget to fill out the card in the back of this book. We want to send you a special certificate for helping us dig up the truth. Now as we gather around the campfire one last time, say Psalm 139:13-14 out loud and really mean it! God loves you and we love you. See you real soon.

Molly, Max, and

(Sam)

P.S. We have some other fun adventures in inductive Bible studies for you to do:

Wrong Way, Jonah! (Jonah)

Jesus in the Spotlight (John 1–10)

Jesus—Awesome Power, Awesome Love (John 11–16)

Jesus—To Eternity and Beyond! (John 17–21)

Boy, Have I Got Problems! (James)

How to Study Your Bible for Kids

PUZZLE ANSWERS

Page 12

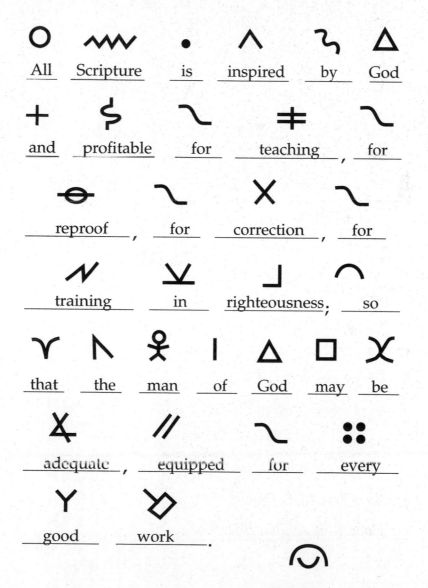

All Scripture is inspired by God and profitable for teaching, for reproof, for correction, for training in righteousness, so that the man of God may be adequate, equipped for every good work.

2 Timothy 3:16-17

Page 28

In the beginning

God created the

heavens and the

earth.

Genesis 1:1

Page 35

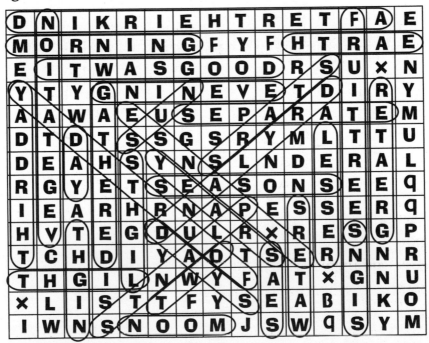

Pages 42-43

1. God created.
2. God was moving.
3. God said.
4. God saw.
5. God separated.
6. God called.
7. God made.
8. God placed.
9. God blessed.
10. God completed.
11. God rested.
12. God sanctified.

Pages 51-52

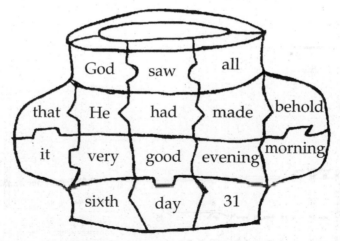

God saw all that He had
made, and behold, it was very
good. And there was evening
and there was morning, the sixth
day.

Genesis 1:31

Page 53

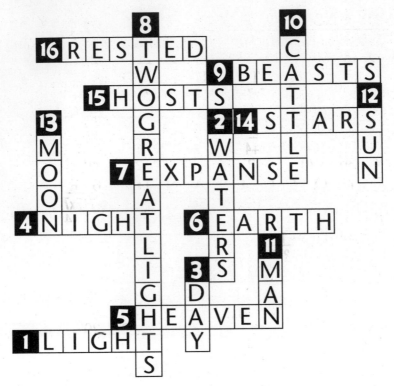

Page 56

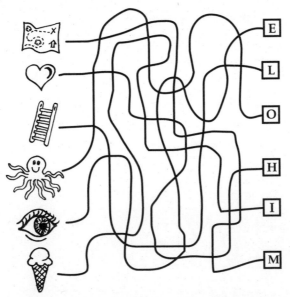

Page 78

T	H	I	S		I	S		T	H	E		D	A	Y
5x7	5+4	3x5	40-10		7+8	5x6		7x5	6+3	24-10		2x6	3+3	5x12
35	9	15	30		15	30		35	9	14		12	6	60

W	H	I	C	H		T	H	E		L	O	R	D
5x10	10-1	3x5	5+5	3x3		5x7	8+1	16-2		24+3	4x9	5x5	7+5
50	9	15	10	9		35	9	14		27	36	25	12

H	A	S		M	A	D	E;	L	E	T		U	S
12-3	4+2	5x6		10+10	2x3	8+4	28-14	3x9	2x7	5x7		20+20	5x6
9	6	30		20	6	12	14	27	14	35		40	30

R	E	J	O	I	C	E		A	N	D		B	E
5x5	10+4	3x7	40-4	3x5	7+3	2x7		5+1	4x7	2x6		10-2	2x7
25	14	21	36	15	10	14		6	28	12		8	14

G	L	A	D		I	N		I	T.
9+9	3x9	7-1	10+2		3x5	4x7		10+5	5x7
18	27	6	12		15	28		15	35

P	S	A	L	M	118:24
4x11	15+15	8-2	3x9	4x5	
44	30	6	27	20	

Page 97

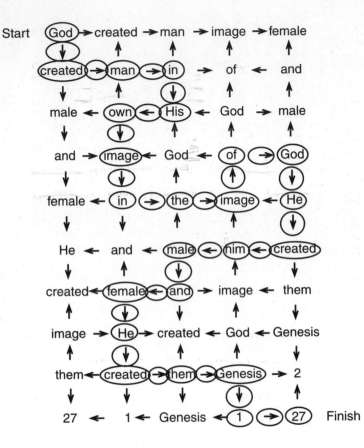

Page 117

For	You	~~quartz~~	~~sand~~	formed
my	~~mica~~	~~slate~~	inward	parts
~~gypsum~~	You	wove	~~clay~~	me
in	my	~~salt~~	mother's	~~mud~~
~~silt~~	womb	~~flint~~	I	~~sandstone~~
will	~~shale~~	give	~~graphite~~	thanks
~~marble~~	to	~~mud~~	You	~~granite~~
for	I	~~silt~~	~~quartz~~	am
fearfully	~~gypsum~~	and	wonderfully	~~clay~~
~~salt~~	made	wonderful	~~mica~~	are
~~shale~~	Your	~~marble~~	works	~~slate~~
and	~~clay~~	my	~~sand~~	soul
~~mica~~	knows	~~granite~~	it	~~flint~~
~~graphite~~	very	~~sandstone~~	well	~~silt~~
~~sand~~	Psalm	139:	~~salt~~	13-14

For You formed my inward parts;

You wove me in my mother's

womb. I will give thanks to You

for I am fearfully and

wonderfully made; wonderful

are Your works, and my

soul knows it very well.

Psalm 139:13-14

Observation Worksheets
GENESIS 1-5

Chapter 1

1 In the beginning God created the heavens and the earth.

2 The earth was formless and void, and darkness was over the surface of the deep, and the Spirit of God was moving over the surface of the waters.

3 Then God said, "Let there be light"; and there was light.

4 God saw that the light was good; and God separated the light from the darkness.

5 God called the light day, and the darkness He called night. And there was evening and there was morning, one day.

6 Then God said, "Let there be an expanse in the midst of the waters, and let it separate the waters from the waters."

7 God made the expanse, and separated the waters which were below the expanse from the waters which were above the expanse; and it was so.

8 God called the expanse heaven. And there was evening and there was morning, a second day.

9 Then God said, "Let the waters below the heavens be gathered into one place, and let the dry land appear"; and it was so.

10 God called the dry land earth, and the gathering of the waters He called seas; and God saw that it was good.

11 Then God said, "Let the earth sprout vegetation: plants yielding

seed, *and* fruit trees on the earth bearing fruit after their kind with

seed in them"; and it was so.

12 The earth brought forth vegetation, plants yielding seed after

their kind, and trees bearing fruit with seed in them, after their

kind; and God saw that it was good.

13 There was evening and there was morning, a third day.

14 Then God said, "Let there be lights in the expanse of the heav-

ens to separate the day from the night, and let them be for signs

and for seasons and for days and years;

15 and let them be for lights in the expanse of the heavens to give

light on the earth"; and it was so.

16 God made the two great lights, the greater light to govern the

day, and the lesser light to govern the night; *He made* the stars also.

17 God placed them in the expanse of the heavens to give light on

the earth,

18 and to govern the day and the night, and to separate the light

from the darkness; and God saw that it was good.

19 There was evening and there was morning, a fourth day.

20 Then God said, "Let the waters teem with swarms of living crea-

tures, and let birds fly above the earth in the open expanse of the

heavens."

21 God created the great sea monsters and every living creature that moves, with which the waters swarmed after their kind, and every winged bird after its kind; and God saw that it was good.

22 God blessed them, saying, "Be fruitful and multiply, and fill the waters in the seas, and let birds multiply on the earth."

23 There was evening and there was morning, a fifth day.

24 Then God said, "Let the earth bring forth living creatures after their kind: cattle and creeping things and beasts of the earth after their kind"; and it was so.

25 God made the beasts of the earth after their kind, and the cattle after their kind, and everything that creeps on the ground after its kind; and God saw that it was good.

26 Then God said, "Let Us make man in Our image, according to Our likeness; and let them rule over the fish of the sea and over the birds of the sky and over the cattle and over all the earth, and over every creeping thing that creeps on the earth."

27 God created man in His own image, in the image of God He created him; male and female He created them.

28 God blessed them; and God said to them, "Be fruitful and multiply, and fill the earth, and subdue it; and rule over the fish of the sea and over the birds of the sky and over every living thing that moves on the earth."

29 Then God said, "Behold, I have given you every plant yielding

seed that is on the surface of all the earth, and every tree which has

fruit yielding seed; it shall be food for you;

30 and to every beast of the earth and to every bird of the sky and

to every thing that moves on the earth which has life, *I have given*

every green plant for food"; and it was so.

31 God saw all that He had made, and behold, it was very good.

And there was evening and there was morning, the sixth day.

Chapter 2

1 Thus the heavens and the earth were completed, and all
their hosts.

2 By the seventh day God completed His work which He had

done, and He rested on the seventh day from all His work which

He had done.

3 Then God blessed the seventh day and sanctified it, because in it

He rested from all His work which God had created and made.

4 This is the account of the heavens and the earth when they were

created, in the day that the LORD God made earth and heaven.

5 Now no shrub of the field was yet in the earth, and no plant of

the field had yet sprouted, for the LORD God had not sent rain upon

the earth, and there was no man to cultivate the ground.

6 But a mist used to rise from the earth and water the whole surface of the ground.

7 Then the LORD God formed <u>man</u> of dust from the ground, and breathed into his nostrils the breath of life; and <u>man</u> became a living being.

8 The LORD God planted a garden toward the east, in Eden; and there He placed the <u>man</u> whom He had formed.

9 Out of the ground the LORD God caused to grow every tree that is pleasing to the sight and good for food; the tree of life also in the midst of the garden, and the tree of the knowledge of good and evil.

10 Now a river flowed out of Eden to water the garden; and from there it divided and became four rivers.

11 The name of the first is Pishon; it flows around the whole land of Havilah, where there is gold.

12 The gold of that land is good; the bdellium and the onyx stone are there.

13 The name of the second river is Gihon; it flows around the whole land of Cush.

14 The name of the third river is Tigris; it flows east of Assyria. And the fourth river is the Euphrates.

15 Then the LORD God took the man and put him into the garden of

Eden to cultivate it and keep it.

16 The LORD God commanded the man, saying, "From any tree of

the garden you may eat freely;

17 but from the tree of the knowledge of good and evil you shall

not eat, for in the day that you eat from it you will surely die."

18 Then the LORD God said, "It is not good for the man to be alone;

I will make him a helper suitable for him."

19 Out of the ground the LORD God formed every beast of the field

and every bird of the sky, and brought *them* to the man to see what

he would call them; and whatever the man called a living creature,

that was its name.

20 The man gave names to all the cattle, and to the birds of the sky,

and to every beast of the field, but for Adam there was not found

helper suitable for him.

21 So the LORD God caused a *deep* sleep to fall upon the man, and

he slept; then He took one of his ribs and closed up the flesh at that

place.

22 The LORD God fashioned into a woman the rib which He had

taken from the man, and brought her to the man.

23 The man said, "This is now bone of my bones, and flesh of my flesh; She shall be called Woman, because she was taken out of Man."

24 For this reason a man shall leave his father and his mother, and be joined to his wife; and they shall become one flesh.

25 And the man and his wife were both naked and were not ashamed.

Chapter 3

1 Now the serpent was more crafty than any beast of the field which the LORD God had made. And he said to the woman, "Indeed, has God said, 'You shall not eat from any tree of the garden'?"

2 The woman said to the serpent, "From the fruit of the trees of the garden we may eat;

3 but from the fruit of the tree which is in the middle of the garden, God has said, 'You shall not eat from it or touch it, or you will die.'"

4 The serpent said to the woman, "You surely will not die!

5 "For God knows that in the day you eat from it your eyes will be opened, and you will be like God, knowing good and evil."

6 When the woman saw that the tree was good for food, and that it was a delight to the eyes, and that the tree was desirable to make

one wise, she took from its fruit and ate; and she gave also to her husband with her, and he ate.

7 Then the eyes of both of them were opened, and they knew that they were naked; and they sewed fig leaves together and made themselves loin coverings.

8 They heard the sound of the LORD God walking in the garden in the cool of the day, and the man and his wife hid themselves from the presence of the LORD God among the trees of the garden.

9 Then the LORD God called to the man, and said to him, "Where are you?"

10 He said, "I heard the sound of You in the garden, and I was afraid because I was naked; so I hid myself."

11 And He said, "Who told you that you were naked? Have you eaten from the tree of which I commanded you not to eat?"

12 The man said, "The woman whom You gave *to be* with me, she gave me from the tree, and I ate."

13 Then the LORD God said to the woman, "What is this you have done?" And the woman said, "The serpent deceived me, and I ate."

14 The LORD God said to the serpent, "Because you have done this, cursed are you more than all cattle, and more than every beast of the field; on your belly you will go, and dust you will eat all the days of your life;

15 and I will put enmity between you and the woman, and

between your seed and her seed; He shall bruise you on the head,

16 And you shall bruise him on the heel." To the woman He said,

"I will greatly multiply your pain in childbirth, in pain you will

bring forth children; yet your desire will be for your husband, and

he will rule over you."

17 Then to Adam He said, "Because you have listened to the voice

of your wife, and have eaten from the tree about which I command-

ed you, saying, 'You shall not eat from it'; cursed is the ground

because of you; In toil you will eat of it all the days of your life.

18 "Both thorns and thistles it shall grow for you; and you will eat

the plants of the field;

19 by the sweat of your face you will eat bread, till you return to

the ground, because from it you were taken; for you are dust, and

to dust you shall return."

20 Now the man called his wife's name Eve, because she was the

mother of all the living.

21 The LORD God made garments of skin for Adam and his wife,

and clothed them.

22 Then the LORD God said, "Behold, the man has become like one

of Us, knowing good and evil; and now, he might stretch out his

hand, and take also from the tree of life, and eat, and live forever"—

23 therefore the LORD God sent him out from the garden of Eden, to cultivate the ground from which he was taken.

24 So He drove the man out; and at the east of the garden of Eden He stationed the cherubim and the flaming sword which turned every direction to guard the way to the tree of life.

Chapter 4

1 Now the man had relations with his wife Eve, and she conceived and gave birth to Cain, and she said, "I have gotten a manchild with *the help of* the LORD."

2 Again, she gave birth to his brother Abel. And Abel was keeper of flocks, but Cain was a tiller of the ground.

3 So it came about in the course of time that Cain brought an offering to the LORD of the fruit of the ground.

4 Abel, on his part also brought of the firstlings of his flock and of their fat portions. And the LORD had regard for Abel and for his offering;

5 but for Cain and for his offering He had no regard. So Cain became very angry and his countenance fell.

6 Then the LORD said to Cain, "Why are you angry? And why has your countenance fallen?"

7 "If you do well, will not *your countenance* be lifted up? And if you do not do well, sin is crouching at the door; and its desire is for you, but you must master it."

8 Cain told Abel his brother. And it came about when they were in the field, that Cain rose up against Abel his brother and killed him.

9 Then the LORD said to Cain, "Where is Abel your brother?" And he said, "I do not know. Am I my brother's keeper?"

10 He said, "What have you done? The voice of your brother's blood is crying to Me from the ground.

11 "Now you are cursed from the ground, which has opened its mouth to receive your brother's blood from your hand.

12 "When you cultivate the ground, it will no longer yield its strength to you; you will be a vagrant and a wanderer on the earth."

13 Cain said to the LORD, "My punishment is too great to bear!

14 "Behold, You have driven me this day from the face of the ground; and from Your face I will be hidden, and I will be a vagrant and a wanderer on the earth, and whoever finds me will kill me."

15 So the LORD said to him, "Therefore whoever kills Cain, vengeance will be taken on him sevenfold." And the LORD appointed a sign for Cain, so that no one finding him would slay him.

16 Then Cain went out from the presence of the LORD, and settled in the land of Nod, east of Eden.

17 Cain had relations with his wife and she conceived, and gave birth to Enoch; and he built a city, and called the name of the city Enoch, after the name of his son.

18 Now to Enoch was born Irad, and Irad became the father of Mehujael, and Mehujael became the father of Methushael, and Methushael became the father of Lamech.

19 Lamech took to himself two wives: the name of the one was Adah, and the name of the other, Zillah.

20 Adah gave birth to Jabal; he was the father of those who dwell in tents and *have* livestock.

21 His brother's name was Jubal; he was the father of all those who play the lyre and pipe.

22 As for Zillah, she also gave birth to Tubal-cain, the forger of all implements of bronze and iron; and the sister of Tubal-cain was Naamah.

23 Lamech said to his wives, "Adah and Zillah, listen to my voice, you wives of Lamech, give heed to my speech, for I have killed a man for wounding me; And a boy for striking me;

24 if Cain is avenged sevenfold, then Lamech seventy-sevenfold."

25 Adam had relations with his wife again; and she gave birth to a

son, and named him Seth, for, *she said*, "God has appointed me

another offspring in place of Abel, for Cain killed him."

26 To Seth, to him also son was born; and he called his name

Enosh. Then *men* began to call upon the name of the Lord.

Chapter 5

1 This is the book of the generations of Adam. In the day when

God created man, He made him in the likeness of God.

2 He created them male and female, and He blessed them and

named them Man in the day when they were created.

3 When Adam had lived one hundred and thirty years, he became

the father of *a son* in his own likeness, according to his image, and

named him Seth.

4 Then the days of Adam after he became the father of Seth were

eight hundred years, and he had *other* sons and daughters.

5 So all the days that Adam lived were nine hundred and thirty

years, and he died.

6 Seth lived one hundred and five years, and became the father of

Enosh.

7 Then Seth lived eight hundred and seven years after he became

the father of Enosh, and he had *other* sons and daughters.

8 So all the days of Seth were nine hundred and twelve years, and he died.

9 Enosh lived ninety years, and became the father of Kenan.

10 Then Enosh lived eight hundred and fifteen years after he became the father of Kenan, and he had *other* sons and daughters.

11 So all the days of Enosh were nine hundred and five years, and he died.

12 Kenan lived seventy years, and became the father of Mahalalel.

13 Then Kenan lived eight hundred and forty years after he became the father of Mahalalel, and he had *other* sons and daughters.

14 So all the days of Kenan were nine hundred and ten years, and he died.

15 Mahalalel lived sixty-five years, and became the father of Jared.

16 Then Mahalalel lived eight hundred and thirty years after he became the father of Jared, and he had *other* sons and daughters.

17 So all the days of Mahalalel were eight hundred and ninety-five years, and he died.

18 Jared lived one hundred and sixty-two years, and became the father of Enoch.

19 Then Jared lived eight hundred years after he became the father of Enoch, and he had *other* sons and daughters.

20 So all the days of Jared were nine hundred and sixty-two years, and he died.

21 Enoch lived sixty-five years, and became the father of Methuselah.

22 Then Enoch walked with God three hundred years after he became the father of Methuselah, and he had *other* sons and daughters.

23 So all the days of Enoch were three hundred and sixty-five years.

24 Enoch walked with God; and he was not, for God took him.

25 Methuselah lived one hundred and eighty-seven years, and became the father of Lamech.

26 Then Methuselah lived seven hundred and eighty-two years after he became the father of Lamech, and he had *other* sons and daughters.

27 So all the days of Methuselah were nine hundred and sixty-nine years, and he died.

28 Lamech lived one hundred and eighty-two years, and became the father of a son.

29 Now he called his name Noah, saying, "This one will give us rest from our work and from the toil of our hands *arising* from the ground which the LORD has cursed."

30 Then Lamech lived five hundred and ninety-five years after he became the father of Noah, and he had *other* sons and daughters.

31 So all the days of Lamech were seven hundred and seventy-seven years, and he died.

32 Noah was five hundred years old, and Noah became the father of Shem, Ham, and Japheth.

BRING THE WHOLE COUNSEL OF GOD'S WORD TO KIDS!

◄ GENESIS
God's Amazing Creation (Genesis 1–2)
Digging Up the Past (Genesis 3–11)
Abraham, God's Brave Explorer (Genesis 11–25)
Extreme Adventures with God (Genesis 24–36)
Joseph, God's Superhero (Genesis 37–50)

◄ DANIEL
You're a Brave Man, Daniel! (Daniel 1–6)
Fast-Forward to the Future (Daniel 7–12)

◄ JONAH
Wrong Way, Jonah!

◄ GOSPEL OF JOHN
Jesus in the Spotlight (John 1–10)
Jesus—Awesome Power, Awesome Love (John 11–16)
Jesus—To Eternity and Beyond (John 17–21)

◄ JAMES
Boy, Have I Got Problems!

◄ REVELATION
Bible Prophecy for Kids (Revelation 1–7)
A Sneak Peek into the Future (Revelation 8–22)

◄ TOPICAL & SKILLS
God, What's Your Name? (Names of God)
Lord, Teach Me to Pray for Kids
How to Study Your Bible—for Kids

Books in the
New Inductive Study Series